Celebrating
Member Recipes & Projects

Minnetonka, Minnesota

Celebrating Member Recipes & Projects

Mike Vail
Vice President, Product and Business Development

Tom Carpenter
Director of Book Development

Dan Kennedy
Book Production Manager

Heather Koshiol
Senior Book Development Coordinator

Zachary Marell
Book Design and Production

PHOTOGRAPHY
Phil Aarrestad Photography *Commissioned Photography*
Abigail Wyckoff *Food Stylist*
Susan Hammes *Prop & Food Stylist*
Kimberly Coburn *Assistant Food Stylist*
John Keenan *Assistant Photographer*
Ron Essex *Assistant Photographer*

1 2 3 4 5 6 7 8 / 03 02 01 00

ISBN 1-58159-123-3

Handyman Club of America
12301 Whitewater Drive
Minnetonka, MN 55343
www.handymanclub.com

The Handyman Club of America proudly presents this special cookbook edition which includes the personal favorites of your fellow Members. Each recipe has been screened by a cooking professional and edited for clarity. However, we are not able to kitchen-test these recipes and cannot guarantee their outcome, or your safety in their preparation or consumption. Please be advised that any recipes that require the use of dangerous equipment (such as pressure cookers), or potentially unsafe preparation procedures (such as canning and pickling), should be used with caution and safe, healthy practices.

Contents

$\mathcal{I}$ntroduction

Making the most of your free time. Creating memories with family and good friends. Building beautiful projects with your own hands. It all makes life even more enjoyable. And the recipes and projects your friends—fellow Club members—share in this book will help you celebrate all of it.

In *Celebrating Member Recipes & Projects*, HCOA members offer more than 200 of their best recipes. Some recipes have been in the family for generations. Others are potluck, picnic, holiday or game-day favorites. Some recipes are tasty after-school snacks or perennial weeknight meals shared regularly at the family supper table.

But because we're do-it-yourselfers, we went beyond the kitchen. Sprinkled among these special recipes, you'll find projects that members have created and sent to us just for this book. Some projects are linked to the kitchen, others to the backyard. You'll find recreation-related projects and projects that members have just plain enjoyed creating.

GET YOUR JUICES FLOWING

The next time you're brainstorming about what to serve guests at a party, what to bring to the family reunion or what to have for dinner, pull out this volume of specially selected recipes for some wonderful food ideas.

And when you find yourself daydreaming about the next project you can't wait to get started on, browse through this colorful book for some great project ideas that are sure to inspire you.

Celebrate *your* free time: Reward yourself with some delicious food and original do-it-yourself project ideas.

Olive Relish Rounds [page 18]

APPETIZERS
& snacks

These recipes for elegant hors d'oeuvres, scrumptious appetizers and satisfying snacks will give you plenty of ideas either for guests to enjoy or for your family to munch on.

Orange-Flavored Pecans [page 24]

Roasted Garlic & Cheese Spread [page 13]

Crab Cakes

1½ lbs. lump crab

2 green onions, slivered

1 rib celery

⅓ c. red pepper, minced

Old Bay Seasoning to taste

Lemon pepper to taste

Fresh dill to taste

Cayenne pepper to taste

Salt to taste

¼ c. flat leaf parsley

½ c. mashed potatoes

1 egg

2 T. mayonnaise

Saltine crackers, mashed

2 T. Parmesan cheese

Oil for frying

Mix together all ingredients except crackers, Parmesan cheese and oil. Form crab cakes the size you want them and make only about ½ inch thick. Mix cracker crumbs and Parmesan cheese together and pat on both sides of the crab cakes. Sauté in hot oil until crisp and drain on paper towels.

SAUCE:

1 to 2 chipotles, canned or fresh

½ c. mayonnaise

¼ c. sour cream

Lemon pepper

1 T. flat leaf parsley

Salt and pepper to taste

Blend chipotles, mayonnaise, sour cream, lemon pepper, parsley, salt and pepper in a food processor or blender. Serve over crab cakes.

Donna Miller
Collierville, TN

Nacho Beef Dip

2 lbs. ground beef

2 lbs. Velveeta cheese

10½-oz. can cream of mushroom soup

12-oz. jar picante sauce

Brown ground beef; drain well. Add other ingredients, warm and serve on corn chips or use for dip. Note: I use a mild picante sauce, but any strength can be used.

Val Brakhahn
Hastings, NE

Hot Wings à la Fay

4 to 5 lbs. chicken wings

Garlic powder

Salt and pepper

2 large bottles Durkee Red Hot Sauce

1 capful white vinegar

2 T. butter

Put wings on baking sheets. Sprinkle with garlic powder, salt and pepper. Bake at 400°F for 60 to 70 minutes.

While wings are baking, pour hot sauce into slow cooker or large saucepan. Add vinegar and butter. Heat on low.

When wings are cooked to your liking, immediately place into sauce. Wings will be ready in 10 minutes. Simmer for 1 hour if you want them to fall off bones. This will also make them a bit hotter. This sauce also makes a great dip; try it with Cajun fries. Leftovers will not be as tasty or as hot.

Douglas Fay
Longmont, CO

Cheese-Glazed Nuts

1½ c. walnut halves

1 T. butter, melted

¼ tsp. hickory-smoked-flavor salt

¼ tsp. regular salt

¼ c. Parmesan cheese, shredded

Preheat oven to 350°F. Spread nuts in shallow baking pan; bake for 10 minutes. Mix butter and both salts; toss lightly with walnuts. Sprinkle cheese over top and stir. Bake for 3 to 4 minutes or until cheese is melted. Stir to blend and place in serving dish.

Gene Mitchell Bryant
Greensburg, KY

Dad's Summer Sausage

4 yds. unbleached muslin, 36 in. wide. Cut 9-in.-wide strips crosswise. Makes about 14 or 15 sacks. Fold lengthwise and sew the side and one end to form the sacks.

1¼ lbs. salt

4 T. pepper

2 T. saltpeter (find at a pharmacy)

2 T. ground cloves

2 lbs. brown sugar

2 qts. dark brown syrup

50 lbs. hamburger or deer burger

Mix all but the meat together. Place meat in large pan and add mixture to meat, making sure everything is mixed well. Place muslin sacks over end of sausage stuffer. Put meat mixture into stuffer and fill sacks except for last 3 inches. Remove from stuffer and tie securely with twine. When all meat is stuffed, hang in smoke house for about 2 to 3 days, depending how much smoke flavor you like. Remove and hang in a cool place like a basement for about 2 to 2½ weeks or until meat begins to dry to your liking. When ready, remove sacks and slice meat. Enjoy.

Roger & Lynn Pletcher
Elkhart, IN

TV Finishings

This entertainment center (top) was an old TV console. I gutted it and made removable shelves for VCR components and other accessories, as you can see from the picture. Glass doors can go on the front. A big-screen TV sits on top when you get it situated where you want it. The shelves can be lowered or raised by 2-in. increments.

The folding TV tray (bottom) folds to less than 3 in. wide. The tray is made of oak and ⅛-in. oak plywood.

Roy Personius
Carthage, MO

Grilled Shrimp with Bacon

Grilled Shrimp with Bacon

1 lb. (26 to 30 count or 36 to 40 count) raw shrimp

1 lb. bacon

18-oz. bottle thick barbecue sauce

12-oz. can beer

Peel shrimp. Cut bacon slices in half. Empty barbecue sauce into bowl. Wrap bacon around shrimp and use toothpick to hold together. Dip shrimp in barbecue sauce, then put on grill. Cook until bacon is done on one side. Turn shrimp and spoon remaining sauce onto shrimp. Bacon drippings will create flames; spray beer over shrimp to put out flames. Close lid of grill quickly so beer will steam into the shrimp. Note: Don't let anyone sample until they're all done or you won't have any left to put on the table!

Timothy Forrester
Grand Rapids, MI

Hot Cheese Spread

2 (8-oz.) pkgs. cream cheese

¾ lb. sharp cheese, shredded or cubed

½ lb. pimiento cheese

2 T. Worcestershire sauce

1 tsp. red pepper

1 tsp. garlic salt

Chili con carne seasoning

Combine cheeses, Worcestershire sauce, red pepper and garlic salt in large mixer bowl. (Tip: If using large mixer bowl, fill sink with hot water just so it's about 2 inches from top of outside of bowl when you push down on the bowl and it touches the bottom of the sink. This will allow the cheese to melt and will be easier to mix.)

After mixing, form into rolls on waxed paper (about 4 rolls). Chill for about 2 hours. Re-form into rolls. Sprinkle chili con carne seasoning on waxed paper and roll cheese in seasoning to coat. The smaller the rolls the spicier it will be.

Davey Radka Sr.
Hendersonville, TN

Barbecued Beef Balls

SAUCE:

2 c. ketchup

2 T. liquid smoke

1 c. brown sugar

½ tsp. salt

3 lbs. lean ground beef

5-oz. can evaporated milk

1 small onion, minced

2 c. oatmeal

2 eggs

2 tsp. salt

Combine ketchup, liquid smoke, brown sugar and ½ teaspoon salt for sauce; set aside.

Mix ground beef, evaporated milk, onion, oatmeal, eggs and 2 teaspoons salt and form into 1-inch balls. Place in a single layer in baking dish. Cover with sauce and bake for 1 hour at 350°F.

Val Brakhahn
Hastings, NE

Super Nachos

1 lb. ground beef

1 envelope taco seasoning

1-lb. jar cheddar cheese sauce

1 bag tortilla chips

Brown ground beef. Mix in taco seasoning according to directions. Warm cheese in saucepan. Arrange chips on round pizza pan and bake at 350°F for 5 minutes. When chips are warm, add ground beef, cheese sauce and top with whatever you like. Examples: refried beans, lettuce, sour cream, tomatoes or green onions.

April Zurlo
Oak Lawn, IL

WALL-HUNG PLATE RACK

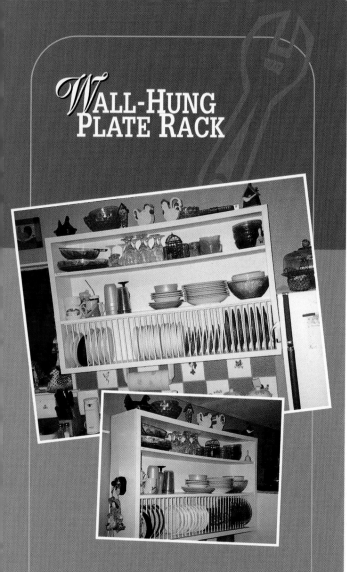

Editor's Note: Vertical plate storage is a great idea that's growing in popularity, and James Bray Sr. of Fresno, California, has captured the concept nicely here. There are several options you could consider for making the vertical rack members: ¼-in. dowels set into guide holes in the lower and middle shelf is the most obvious (try using a strip of pegboard as a drilling guide to get your dowel holes aligned). Or, you could buy a couple of pieces of plastic-coated wire closet shelving and rig them up in a vertical position. Closet shelving is sold in 12 and 16-in. widths. You may need to do a little trimming or remove a crosspiece or two so the plates will clear. To trim the shelving for width, sandwich it in between two strips of plywood, then cut it with a circular saw fitted with a remodeler's blade. One other point: If you add an upper shelf and the cabinet is more than 30 in. wide, insert a vertical shelf divider for support.

James Bray Sr.
Fresno, CA

Artichokes Ramekin
(Or, Artichokes' Armegeddon)

2 (6½-oz.) cans quartered non-marinated artichoke hearts, drained well and cut into smaller pieces

1 fresh jalapeño pepper, finely diced; add more or less to taste

1 c. shredded Parmesan cheese

5-oz. pkg. goat cheese, brought to room temperature (plain chèvre cheese works best)

¼ c. mayonnaise

¼ c. sour cream

Freshly cracked pepper to taste

2 or more cloves garlic to taste, pressed or shredded

Mix artichoke hearts, jalapeño pepper, Parmesan cheese, goat cheese, mayonnaise, sour cream, pepper and garlic together well. (If, after combining, the ingredients still seem dry add a bit more sour cream.) Refrigerate for 2 to 3 hours to allow flavors to blend.

Preheat oven to 400°F. Put mixture in shallow oven-proof dish and bake until top begins turning brown. Do not overcook. Can be served with crackers but is best with baguette.

Camille Rafa
Minneapolis, MN

Deb's Italian Party Dip

8 oz. sour cream

2 tsp. vinegar

5 tsp. cooking oil

1 c. mayonnaise or salad dressing

Pkg. Good Seasons Italian dressing mix

Mix sour cream, vinegar, oil, mayonnaise and Good Seasons mix together and enjoy on chips or crackers.

Rhonda Bahr
Medford, WI

Roasted Garlic & Cheese Spread

1 bulb garlic, unpeeled

1 tsp. olive oil

1¼ c. milk

2 large eggs

1 c. grated Parmesan cheese

1 tsp. grated onion

¼ tsp. white pepper

1 tsp. caraway seed

½ tsp. dried thyme, crushed

Brush unpeeled garlic bulb with olive oil. Wrap bulb in aluminum foil and bake for 30 minutes at 375°F. Remove from oven and cool for 30 minutes. Trim end of garlic, squeeze pulp from bulb into food processor or blender. Add milk, eggs, cheese, onion and pepper. Cover and process until smooth.

Transfer to a greased 8-inch quiche dish or 9-inch pie plate. Sprinkle with caraway seed and thyme. Bake in 375°F oven for 20 to 25 minutes until puffed and lightly browned. Cool for 30 minutes. Cover and refrigerate until thoroughly chilled. Serve with crackers or mini toasts.

Lisa Krajnak
Lyndhurst, OH

Roasted Garlic & Cheese Spread

ENTERTAINMENT ROOM

*O*ur daughter's home had a covered patio bordered by three sides of the house. This configuration presented an ideal opportunity for adding a wall to enclose the area and thereby add an entertainment room for her family. Getting as much sunlight into the house as possible was an objective.

The first step in the process was to raise the floor level to the same height as the rest of the house. Horizontal and vertical rebar was added to tie into the existing structure. The patio had been painted previously, so a good moisture barrier already existed. Horizontal 2 x 4-in. boards were nailed to the three sides of the house. A screed was then moved across these 2 x 4-in. boards to construct a floor at the correct height.

Next, the wall was constructed, with openings for a door and two of the six windows that were removed from existing sides. The opening where the original door existed was closed off. In the opening where the six windows were located, one was closed, one had glass-paned French doors added and one had pass-throughs with counters added. The doors were double paned for outside use, but by using them indoors an excellent sound barrier was created.

The project was completed by adding a ceiling light and fan, inside and outside wall plugs, an outside light, tile at the door, carpet, insulation in the attic, a TV antenna outlet and a phone outlet for the computer.

This was a fun project that should result in many years of enjoyment. It was also an opportunity for my son-in-law to learn many aspects of house construction.

**Gene Schell
Bartonville, TX**

Stuffed Mushrooms

24 large fresh mushrooms

16-oz. pkg. bulk pork sausage

8-oz. pkg. cream cheese

Fresh Parmesan cheese, grated

Wash mushrooms. Remove stems and chop into small pieces. Place mushroom caps on baking sheet. Brown sausage in skillet. Drain.

Add cream cheese and chopped mushroom stems to sausage. Mix well—cream cheese and mushroom stems should be thoroughly combined with sausage. Fill each mushroom cap with spoonful of sausage mixture. Sprinkle with Parmesan cheese. Bake for 15 minutes at 375°F.

Michele Teigen
Monticello, MN

Party Rye Pizza

1 lb. hot sausage

1 lb. Velveeta cheese, cut into chunks

1 to 2 tsp. Italian dressing

1 T. ketchup

Loaf sliced party rye

Cook sausage and drain well, pressing all fat out with paper towels. Add cheese, dressing and ketchup; mix well. Spread mixture on party rye.

Bake at 375°F for 8 to 10 minutes until edges brown. Can use sandwich bread and cut each slice into 4 pieces.

Donna Miller
Collierville, TN

Cheese Bread

1 c. shredded mozzarella cheese

1 c. mayonnaise

1 c. chopped onion

1 loaf French bread, sliced

Oregano to taste

Combine cheese, mayonnaise and onion. Spread mixture on each slice of bread. Sprinkle with oregano. Broil or grill bread until topping is golden brown. Serve warm.

Gary Szepelak
Plantation, FL

Hot Chipped Beef Dip

2 (8-oz.) pkgs. cream cheese

4 T. milk

1 c. sour cream

2 (3-oz.) pkgs. smoked chipped beef, chopped into small pieces

½ c. finely chopped green onion

½ tsp. pepper

½ tsp. garlic salt

Soften cream cheese slightly in microwave. Add milk and sour cream; mix well. Add chipped beef, green onion, pepper and garlic salt; mix well.

Bake for 20 minutes at 350°F. Serve hot with either French bread or tortilla chips.

Shannon Koshiol
Fort Collins, CO

Cocktail Mix

12-oz. box Crispix

12-oz. box Cheerios

1 lb. margarine

1 lb. peanuts

15-oz. bag pretzel sticks

1 T. celery salt

1 T. onion salt

1 T. garlic salt

Place cereals, margarine, peanuts, pretzel sticks and seasonings in a big roaster; mix well and cook at 250°F for 45 minutes, stirring every 15 minutes.

Mark & Tracia Hogue
White, SD

Wild Card Fresh Chive & Bacon Dip

¾ lb. fresh raw bacon slices

1¼ lbs. cream cheese

¼ c. minced red onions

8 oz. sour cream

1 tsp. fresh chopped parsley

½ tsp. A-1 Sauce

1 tsp. fresh raw garlic

½ tsp. Worcestershire sauce

⅛ c. chopped fresh chives

Chop bacon and sauté until fully cooked. Drain on paper towels and cool. Combine ingredients and mix until smooth. Store in airtight container in refrigerator until serving time. Serve in bowl surrounded by a variety of flavored crackers or chips.

Denise Young
Blaine, MN

Goat Cheese, Salami & Tomato Appetizers

20 mini-baguette slices or mini-bagels, toasted lightly

6 oz. soft mild goat cheese

10 slices hard salami, each quartered into triangles

60 slices cherry tomato (about 20 tomatoes)

20 small basil sprigs

Pepper

Spread baguette slices with cheese. Top each half with 2 salami triangles, 3 slices tomato and a basil sprig. Sprinkle toppings lightly with pepper.

Dave Jansen
St. Paul, MN

Pâté

8-oz. pkg. cream cheese

8 oz. braunschweiger

1 T. lemon juice

1 T. Worcestershire sauce

Minced onion to taste

Mix cream cheese, braunschweiger, lemon juice, Worcestershire sauce and onion. Serve with crackers.

Donna Miller
Collierville, TN

Goat Cheese, Salami & Tomato Appetizers

Olive Relish Rounds

Olive Relish Rounds

1 lb. black olives, pitted and finely chopped

1 c. green pimiento-stuffed olives, finely chopped

1 red bell pepper, diced

¼ c. parsley, minced

2 T. minced garlic

2 T. anchovy paste

2 T. fresh oregano, minced

½ c. olive oil

Freshly ground black pepper to taste

Toasted bread rounds

In large bowl, combine black and green olives, red bell pepper, parsley, garlic, anchovy paste, oregano, olive oil and black pepper. Cover and marinate overnight in refrigerator. Serve with toasted bread rounds.

Can be made more than a week in advance and stored in refrigerator with a thin layer of olive oil on top to preserve the color and flavor.

Donna Miller
Collierville, TN

Trail Mix

2 lbs. dry-roasted peanuts

18½-oz. pkg. pretzel chips

17-oz. pkg. thin pretzel twists

5¾-oz. pkg. pretzel sticks

5.6-oz. pkg. Corn Nuts

1 c. vegetable oil

1 c. melted butter

2 T. chili powder

2 T. Worcestershire sauce

5 drops green hot sauce

1 T. garlic salt

1 T. seasoned salt

1 tsp. ground cumin

Chocolate-covered raisins, optional

Mix nuts and pretzels in large roasting pan. Mix oil and melted butter; add chili powder, Worcestershire sauce, hot sauce, garlic salt, seasoned salt and cumin. Mix well. Pour over pretzels and mix well.

Bake at 250°F for 2 hours, stirring often. For variety, add chocolate-covered raisins.

Terry & Donna Nunley
Gruetli, TN

Sausage Balls

3 c. baking mix

1 lb. hot sausage, room temperature

½ lb. sharp cheese, grated

Combine baking mix, sausage and cheese. Mix well and roll into balls. Place in ungreased baking dish. Bake at 450°F for 15 minutes.

Donna Miller
Collierville, TN

LOG CABIN CLOCK

I made this log cabin clock from various things I had lying around the house. It is based on my old home near the Blue Ridge Mountains in Virginia.

The cabin was cut on a scroll saw from a wood scrap. The logs were whittled round to give a 3-dimensional effect. The trim was made from scrap wicker baskets. Rocks along the stream are redwood mulch chips. The trees were made with trimmings from a juniper bush. Various acrylic paints were used for coloring the stream, landscaping, mountains and a couple of trees in the background.

Jimmy Lofton
Via e-mail

Beef Jerky à la Fay

2 T. soy sauce

2 c. water

2 T. liquid smoke

4 T. Worcestershire sauce

½ c. brown sugar

3 T. onion salt

3 T. hot pepper sauce

1 T. black pepper

1½ to 2 lbs. top round steak (London broil or top sirloin)

Mix soy sauce, water, liquid smoke, Worcestershire sauce, brown sugar, onion salt, pepper sauce and pepper. Trim all fat from meat and slice against the grain to ⅛ to ¼ inch thick. Marinate in soy sauce mixture for 8 hours, stirring and turning occasionally.

Drain meat on paper towels, place on foil over oven grate, sprinkle lightly with black pepper. Place rack in center of oven, and set heat to lowest possible setting, leaving door slightly ajar. Note: Some ovens will not go low enough and will dry the meat too quickly, causing it to be brittle.

Bake for approximately 10 hours. Turn and dry for 5 to 10 hours more, depending on size of pieces, and remove smaller pieces, testing the others occasionally to prevent overdrying. Must be thoroughly dried without becoming tough or brittle.

Remove jerky and put into zip-top bags. Freeze portions not to be used within the first week. Will have a spicy, slightly teriyaki taste. Adjust seasonings as desired after initial batch. Note any changes for future reference. A world-class jerky!

Douglas Fay
Longmont, CO

Maple Cinnamon Granola

2 lbs. rolled oats, not instant

1 c. raw, hulled sunflower seeds

½ c. sweetened, flaked coconut

1 tsp. ground cinnamon

2 c. raisins

2 cups your favorite roasted nuts (peanuts, almonds, etc.)

3 T. water

½ tsp. salt

1 c. maple syrup (real is best, but may use pancake type)

½ c. vegetable oil

1 tsp. vanilla

In large bowl, combine oats, sunflower seeds, coconut, cinnamon, raisins and nuts. Heat water and salt in small saucepan until salt dissolves, then add syrup and oil; bring to simmer.

Remove from heat, then whisk in vanilla and pour over oat mixture. Toss until all of oats mixture is covered and evenly moist. Roast granola for 45 minutes at 300°F until cooked evenly. Allow to cool in the pans, then break up and store in sealed plastic bags.

Kelly Kutz
St. Petersburg, FL

Broccoli Dip

⅔ c. powdered broccoli soup mix

8 oz. sour cream

Dash of garlic salt

Dash of pepper

Combine soup mix, sour cream, garlic salt and pepper. Serve in hollowed-out Hawaiian bread loaf or with crackers.

Donna Miller
Collierville, TN

DECORATIVE GOLF-CLUB LAMPS

I've seen golf-club lamps like the ones I've made offered for sale for hundreds of dollars. But being an avid do-it-yourselfer, golfer, handyman and partial cheapskate, I decided to try my own hand at making them. I believe I ended up with a project that is superior in quality and one that can be had at an affordable price. The used golf clubs were found at yard sales and flea markets for only a few dollars. The lampshade was the most expensive component.

Visitors to our home are impressed by the uniqueness of the lamps—many golfing friends have insisted on one for themselves. As a matter of fact, I've been told I should be making these lamps to sell!

Dean Weaver
Abbottstown, PA

BLT Dip

1 c. mayonnaise or salad dressing

2 c. sour cream

2 lbs. bacon, cooked and crumbled

1 large tomato, chopped

1 green onion, chopped, optional

1 loaf bread, slices toasted and cut into 4 triangles

Mix mayonnaise, sour cream, bacon, tomato and onion in bowl. Chill in refrigerator for at least 4 hours (overnight is even better). Serve on toast. Leftovers make good sandwiches.

April Zurlo
Oak Lawn, IL

Steven's Wings

5-lb. bag chicken wings

4 (12-oz.) bottles Red Hot

1 pkg. Shake 'n Bake Herb & Garlic Perfect Potatoes

½ c. butter

Broil, bake or grill wings until skin is crispy and juices run clear. Meanwhile in cooking pot, combine Red Hot, Shake 'n Bake and butter. Cook over medium heat until butter is melted and Shake 'n Bake is completely incorporated. Add wings and coat with sauce. Serve with carrots, celery and blue cheese or ranch dressing.

Steven Carroll
Franklin, MA

BLT Dip

Steven's Wings

Orange-Flavored Pecans

1 c. sugar

⅓ c. orange juice

2 T. grated orange peel

1½ c. pecan halves

Cook sugar, orange juice and orange peel in large saucepan, stirring constantly, to 230°F on candy thermometer (will form a 2-inch soft thread when spoon is lifted above pan). Add pecan halves. Stir until mixture turns to white crystals and nuts cling together.

Remove from pan to baking sheet covered in waxed paper. Try to separate pecans with spoon. Will separate easily when cooled.

Donna Miller
Collierville, TN

Orange-Flavored Pecans

Tom's Roasted Red Bell Peppers

4 to 6 large red bell peppers

Light virgin olive oil

¼ clove garlic

Salt and freshly ground pepper to taste

Stand peppers in baking dish and bake at 400°F. Remove from oven when tops of peppers are black. Cool to room temperature.

Remove stems and seeds. Cut peppers in half and remove skin. Clean out all seeds and pat dry. Mix oil and garlic in bowl or deep dish. Add peppers. Let stand for 3 hours. Serve cold or warm.

Tom Cane
Norristown, PA

Barbecue Li'l Smokies

1 lb. Little Smokies

2 c. favorite barbecue sauce

¼ c. cola

1 T. Tabasco sauce

Mix sausages, barbecue sauce, cola and Tabasco sauce in slow cooker and cook for 1 to 2 hours on low to medium.

Wayne Roberts
McCalla, AL

Virtual "Scrumby Dippage"

2 hard-cooked eggs

¾-oz. pkg. Uncle Dan's Southern Dressing Mix

1 c. mayonnaise

8 oz. sour cream

4¼-oz. can tiny shrimp or crabmeat, drained (or fresh if available)

2 to 3 shakes of dry dill weed, or to taste

Pepper to taste

Smash eggs in bowl with fork. Add dressing mix, mayonnaise, sour cream, shrimp or crabmeat, dill weed and pepper; mix well. Chill in refrigerator until ready to use as dip.

Len Zuvela
Everett, WA

Hot Spinach & Artichoke Dip

10-oz. pkg. frozen spinach, thawed

6½-oz. can small artichoke hearts, chopped

1 c. mozzarella cheese, divided

1 c. Parmesan cheese, divided

1 T. lemon juice

In 9 x 9-inch baking dish, mix spinach, artichoke hearts, ¾ cup mozzarella cheese, ¾ cup Parmesan cheese and lemon juice. Top with remaining cheeses. Bake at 350°F for 30 minutes. Serve with blue tortilla chips.

Angela Heltemes
Champlin, MN

Wing Sauces

Suicide Sauce

12-oz. jar habanero peppers

12-oz. jar jalapeño peppers

½ gal. Franks Red Hot Sauce

1 c. (2 sticks) margarine

2 c. red pepper flakes

1 c. cayenne pepper

1 c. cajun seasoning

¼ c. black pepper

¼ c. garlic powder

40 lbs. wings

Blend peppers and juice from jars. Combine all ingredients in a pot and cook until hot. Dip fried wings in sauce. Be ready to grab a slice of bread and a couple of glasses of milk!

Mild Sauce

4 c. (8 sticks or ½-gal. tub) margarine or butter

½ gal. Frank's Red Hot Sauce

40 lbs. wings

Put margarine in a pot. Add hot sauce. Cook until hot. If sauce is too spicy, add more margarine. Meanwhile, fry wings. Dip cooked wings in heated sauce.

Garlic Parmesan

4 c. (8 sticks or ½-gal. tub) margarine or butter

1 c. minced garlic

½ c. garlic powder

½ c. granulated garlic

½ to ¾ c. Parmesan cheese

40 lbs. wings

Melt margarine. Add remaining ingredients and mix well. Dip fried wings in sauce.

Buffalo Sauce

6 to 10 (14-oz.) bottles ketchup

1 c. red pepper flakes

8 c. sugar

4 c. water

4 c. apple cider vinegar

8 T. prepared mustard

3 dashes of Worcestershire sauce

40 lbs. wings

Combine all ingredients, mix well and bring to a boil. Stir occasionally while boiling. Boil for about 5 minutes. Let simmer for 10 to 15 minutes. Dip fried wings in sauce. Dip grilled chicken breast in sauce and place on a kaiser bun, then pour blue cheese dressing on top for a good sandwich!

Todd Fritz
Pittsburgh, PA

Curried Pecans

3½ tsp. sugar

1½ tsp. curry powder

1 tsp. salt

½ c. pecan halves

5 T. olive oil

Mix sugar, curry powder and salt. Place pecans on baking sheet; sprinkle with oil and spices. Bake at 275°F for 30 minutes, stirring every 10 minutes.

Nuts will keep well for 2 to 3 weeks if stored in airtight container.

Donna Miller
Collierville, TN

Super Thick Nacho Dip

1 lb. sausage

1 lb. ground beef

14-oz. can diced tomatoes and green chiles

10¾-oz..can cream of mushroom soup

1 lb. Velveeta cheese, cut into chunks

Cook sausage in Dutch oven. Add ground beef and cook until browned. Drain grease from pan.

Add tomatoes and soup; stir thoroughly. Add cheese chunks and continue stirring until cheese is melted. Serve hot with sturdy tortilla chips.

Kevin Frey
Gardner, KS

Custom Doghouse

Using the idea for a doghouse published in your *Outdoor Woodworking Projects* book, I built this doghouse for a Labrador pup. This house measures 65 in. long x 40 in. high. The dog loves it and enjoys the breezeway.

Paul Durr
Fairborn, OH

Mexican Appetizers

Mexican Appetizers

1 large pizza crust
½ c. chopped red pepper
½ c. chopped yellow pepper
½ c. chopped green pepper
½ to ¾ c. light sour cream
1½ c. colby-jack cheese
¼ c. chopped cilantro

Place pizza crust on baking sheet. Combine all peppers, sour cream and cheese. Spread sour cream mixture on crust almost to edge. Bake at 375°F for 25 to 30 minutes.

Sprinkle with cilantro. Let stand for about 10 minutes. Cut into wedges and serve with chunky salsa.

Char Salzbrun
Coon Rapids, MN

Beefy Roll-Ups

8-oz. pkg. cream cheese
½ c. mayonnaise
½ c. sour cream
2 T. Dijon mustard
¼ c. green onion, chopped
1 tsp. dill weed
½ tsp. minced garlic
¼ tsp. pepper
12 (10-in.) flour tortillas
Leaf lettuce
2 lbs. seasoned deli-style roast beef

Soften cream cheese; combine with mayonnaise, sour cream, mustard, green onion and seasonings. Spread mixture over tortillas. Layer cheese mixture with leaf lettuce and beef. Roll up.

Chill for 1 hour or longer. Slice into 2-inch pinwheels.

Carol Arndt
Roseville, MN

Beefy Roll-Ups

Holiday Popcorn

14 c. popped corn, or 2 microwave bags of popped corn, unpopped kernels removed

3 c. Razzle Dazzle (colored) Rice Krispies cereal

2 c. salted nuts

1 lb. white or butterscotch almond bark

3 T. peanut butter

Place popped corn, cereal and nuts in large kettle. Melt almond bark and peanut butter in microwave dish and pour over popcorn mixture. Mix well. Let rest on waxed paper or on 2 large pans for 2 hours. Store covered.

Juanita Angell
Elkton, MN

Vidalia Onion Dip

2 c. Vidalia onion or any sweet onion

2 c. mayonnaise, regular or light

2 c. shredded Swiss cheese

Preheat oven to 375°F. Mix ingredients together in bowl. Pour into 8 x 8-inch baking dish or casserole pan. Bake at 375°F for 30 minutes, checking often, until lightly browned and bubbling. Be careful! It will be very hot when it comes out of the oven. Give it a few minutes to cool down. Serve with crackers or toasted rounds of French bread.

Donna Miller
Collierville, TN

Italian Stuffed Zucchini

1 slice bread

Milk

1 lb. zucchini, unpeeled

3 fresh mushrooms, chopped

¼ c. bread crumbs, divided

2 slices bacon, fried crisp and chopped

¼ c. grated Parmesan cheese, divided

1 tsp. Italian seasoning

Black pepper

1 egg

Olive oil

Remove crust from bread and soak in saucer of milk for 5 minutes. Squeeze dry. Place zucchini in salted boiling water for 3 minutes. Drain. Cut each in half lengthwise. Scoop out soft center with teaspoon.

Place scooped-out zucchini centers in bowl with mushrooms, ⅛ cup breadcrumbs, soaked bread, bacon, ⅛ cup Parmesan cheese, Italian seasoning and a pinch of black pepper. Mix together.

Beat egg smoothly and blend with mixture. Fill zucchini halves with mixture and place on lightly oiled baking sheet. Brush olive oil over them. Mix together ⅛ cup breadcrumbs and ⅛ cup Parmesan cheese. Sprinkle mixture over tops of zucchini.

Bake at 350°F for 30 minutes. Great served hot or cold.

Gary Mallon
Post Falls, ID

Nancy's Favorite Chip Dip

8 oz. sour cream

8 oz. shredded cheddar cheese

8 oz. chunky salsa

Mix sour cream, cheese and salsa. Serve with corn chips.

Nancy Skordahl
Blaine, MN

OUTDOOR PLAY CENTER

My house is on a semi-busy street. The front yard is small and the back yard slopes all the way down to the property line. My wife and I were concerned about our boys playing in the front yard because of the traffic, but there was no flat area to play in the back. My solution to this problem was to start what ended up being a two-year project. I framed in an area 12½ ft. x 10 ft. and filled it with waste rock, topped with pea gravel. Then I replaced a window in the dining room with a sliding patio door and built a 10-ft. x 20-ft. deck. The deck is supported by two 4-in. x 6-in. beams and outer 4-in. x 4-in. posts. The deck is not connected to the house.

To complete the project, I built a 6-ft. x 8-ft. playhouse near the deck. The railings match the deck and the roof is very steep with sheathing and shingles, just like a house would have. I added a suspended bridge between the deck and the playhouse. This is currently the only way into the playhouse. An attached slide gives an exit out of the playhouse. A merry-go-round and swings were also added to the playhouse. The lower part of the playhouse is closed in with heavy-duty lattice and it has a 10-in.-deep layer of sand for an additional play area.

Building this project has been an enjoyable experience for me as well as a learning experience for my boys, who helped on most of the project in some way.

Gary Duncan
Fayett, MO

Easy Pickled Eggs

Onion, sliced

½ tsp. celery seed

2 bay leaves

1 tsp. salt

2 T. sugar

Water

Vinegar

12 hard-cooked eggs, peeled

In 2-quart jar, place onion, celery seed, bay leaves, salt and sugar. Pour in 1 cup water and 1 cup vinegar. Shake in covered jar to mix ingredients. Add eggs and top off jar with additional vinegar. Refrigerate for 2 to 3 days before serving.

Rhonda Bahr
Medford, WI

Deluxe Deviled Eggs

4 hard-cooked eggs

1 T. blue cheese

1 tsp. yellow mustard

1 tsp. finely chopped green onions

½ tsp. dried rosemary

2 tsp. mayonnaise or salad dressing

1 tsp. salt

½ tsp. pepper

Paprika or ground red pepper

Mix egg yolks, cheese, mustard, onion, rosemary, mayonnaise and salt until fluffy. Stuff the whites with yolk mixture and sprinkle with paprika or red pepper.

Kelly Kutz
St. Petersburg, FL

Catalina Smokies

1 lb. Little Smokies

8-oz. bottle Catalina French Dressing

Place Smokies in a slow cooker. Pour dressing over them. Cook on low for approximately 2 hours for flavor to blend.

Val Brakhahn
Hastings, NE

Party Mix

12-oz. box Cheerios

12-oz. box Rice Chex

12-oz. box Corn or Wheat Chex

10-oz. bag pretzels

½ lb. butter, melted

½ lb. margarine, melted

½ tsp. garlic salt or 1 T. seasoned salt

2 T. Worcestershire sauce

12 oz. cocktail peanuts

Mix cereals and pretzels together. In separate bowl, mix melted butter, margarine, salt and Worcestershire sauce. Pour sauce over cereal mixture a little at a time and stir well. Bake for 1½ hours at 250°F. Stir occasionally. Add peanuts and bake for ½ hour longer. Cool. Ready to serve immediately. Note: A large roasting pan works best for this recipe.

Tim & Nicole Lebakken
Galesville, WI

Mango Salsa

4 mangos, diced

3 Roma tomatoes, diced

1 medium red onion, finely chopped

2 jalapeño peppers, finely chopped

1 green bell pepper, chopped

1 red bell pepper, chopped

1 yellow bell pepper, chopped

4 cloves fresh garlic, or 3 T. chopped garlic

2 to 3 Mandarin oranges

Fresh cilantro to taste

Mix mangos, tomatoes, onion, all peppers, garlic and oranges in large bowl. Refrigerate before serving.

Tip: For best results, use mangos that are just starting to go soft.

Kurt Richter
Gretna, LA

Mexican Chip Dip

2 (10½-oz.) cans jalapeño bean dip

2 c. ripe avocado, mashed

1 T. lemon juice

½ tsp. seasoned salt

1½ c. sour cream, divided

½ c. mayonnaise

1 envelope taco seasoning mix

4 oz. shredded cheddar cheese

1 small tomato, chopped

½ c. sliced ripe black olives

¼ c. chopped green onions

Spread bean dip over bottom of 10-inch pie plate. Combine avocado, lemon juice and seasoned salt. Spread over bean dip. Combine 1 cup sour cream, mayonnaise and taco seasoning. Spread over avocado layer. Beat remaining sour cream. Carefully spread on top. Sprinkle with cheese, tomato, olives and onions.

Chill for 1 hour. Serve with tortilla chips.

Margaret Tchida
St. Cloud, MN

Fresh Chive & Bacon Dip

¾ lb. fresh, raw bacon

1¼ lbs. cream cheese

¼ c. minced red onion

8 oz. sour cream

1 tsp. chopped fresh parsley

½ tsp. A-1 sauce

1 tsp. chopped fresh garlic

½ tsp. Worcestershire sauce

⅛ c. fresh chives, cut

Chop bacon. Cook in sauté pan until fully cooked, drain on paper towels and cool. In a mixing bowl, mix all ingredients until smooth. Store in airtight container in refrigerator until serving time. Serve in a bowl surrounded by a variety of flavored crackers or chips.

Donna Miller
Collierville, TN

Spinach Dip

10-oz. pkg. frozen spinach, thawed

1 pkg. dry vegetable soup mix

1 c. sour cream

1 c. real mayonnaise (not salad dressing)

1 medium onion, chopped

1 loaf Hawaiian bread

Place spinach in bowl. Separate soup vegetables from soup mix using a strainer over spinach in bowl. Run hot water over vegetables from soup mix for 3 minutes. Mix seasoned spinach, sour cream, mayonnaise and onion and add vegetables from soup mix. Chill dip for 2 hours.

Hollow out center of bread and put dip in center. Use pieces from center for dipping.

Angela Heltemes
Champlin, MN

ROOM DIVIDER PANELS

Nowadays, in our little corner of the world, "leisure time" usually is relaxing in a quiet corner in a comfortable rocking chair with a good book. A folding screen/room divider allows privacy and keeps the light out of the rest of the bedroom if some-one is asleep. It's perfect for a computer nook, writing, reading, television and even for a baby crib.

We saw a similar folding screen/divider in an antique mall and decided to make our own as a project for our newly remodeled vacation home. We used knotty pine and contrasting walnut for the wood. The fabric used matches the reupholstered old rocker (a gift of many years ago from my father). The fabric panels are removable at the top so they can be changed. The back of the screen has paintings, plaques and family photos on it for interest. We get lots of compliments on it.

**Glen Fulcher
Seattle, WA**

Cheese Roll

8-oz. pkg. cream cheese, room temperature

1 lb. shredded sharp cheddar cheese, room temperature

2 tsp. Worcestershire sauce

1 tsp. Tabasco sauce

½ tsp. garlic powder

Cayenne pepper to taste

Paprika

Mix cheeses, Worcestershire sauce, Tabasco sauce, garlic powder and cayenne pepper and roll in paprika.

Donna Miller
Collierville, TN

Turkey Spam & Cheese Spread

12-oz. can Turkey Spam, grated

½ c. American cheese, grated

1 T. finely chopped hot peppers, optional

½ c. mayonnaise

Combine Spam, cheese, hot peppers and mayonnaise. Mix well and shape into a ball. Serve with crackers.

Natalie Brock
Shreveport, LA

Sweet Nuts & Bolts

16-oz. box Quaker Oat Squares cereal

2 c. pecan pieces

½ c. light corn syrup

½ c. firmly packed brown sugar

¼ c. margarine

1 tsp. vanilla

½ tsp. baking soda

Preheat oven to 250°F. Combine cereal and pecans in 9 x 13-inch pan. Set aside. Combine corn syrup, brown sugar and margarine in 2-cup microwaveable bowl. Microwave on high for ½ to 1½ minutes. Stir.

Microwave on high for ½ to 1½ minutes more until boiling. Stir in vanilla and baking soda and pour over cereal mixture. Stir to coat evenly.

Bake for 1 hour, stirring every 20 minutes. Spread on baking sheet to cool. Break into pieces.

Donna Miller
Collierville, TN

Easy Salsa Dip

1 lb. sour cream

8 oz. salsa (hot, medium or mild)

8 oz. shredded cheddar cheese

Spread sour cream on bottom of medium bowl or serving plate. Pour salsa on top of sour cream and spread evenly. Top with cheddar to make top layer. Serve with tortilla chips.

James D. Mullen
East Meredith, NY

Beautiful Soup [page 47]

Focaccia [page 47]

SOUPS & SALADS
sides & breads

These pages include soups and breads that will warm you from the inside out, side dishes to serve with any dinner, and cool salads that are perfect for serving on hot summer days.

Greek Salad Dressing [page 42]

Custom Display Cases

I built these display cases to show off our scale model trains. I used solid oak and ¼-in. oak plywood. All the cases are 24 in. tall and 3½ in. deep; some are 44 in. long and the others are 60 in. long. There are four shelves in each. They have ⅛-in. grooves about ½ in. apart for the wheel flanges.

The corners and back pieces use rabbet joints and the shelves fit against the sides with butt joints. The shelves are also screwed in from behind. I used ⅛-in.-thick Plexiglas on the front, set into grooves. I applied a danish oil finish. I've made three small ones and two big ones so far.

Paul Quibell
San Francisco, CA

Wild Rice Soup

1 lb. wild rice
½ c. brown rice
1 large onion
1 c. celery
1 lb. mushrooms
½ c. butter
¼ tsp. Mrs. Dash
⅛ tsp. pepper
1 c. flour
16 c. chicken broth
2 boneless, skinless chicken breasts
½ lb. ham
1 pt. half-and-half

Soak wild rice and brown rice overnight. Rinse thoroughly and cook until tender. Drain and rinse thoroughly again. Set aside.

While rice is cooking, cut up onion, celery and mushrooms; sauté in butter until tender. Add Mrs. Dash and pepper. Add flour and stir until butter is soaked up and vegetables are coated with flour.

In large pot, heat chicken broth. Add sautéed vegetables and stir with wire whisk until flour coating has been dissolved in broth. Stir in rice.

Cut up chicken breasts and cook thoroughly. Stir into soup. Cut up ham and stir into soup. Add half-and-half to regulate the thickness of soup.

Soup is now ready to eat. I usually simmer soup for a couple of hours to promote maximum taste. In fact, if you refrigerate it overnight and reheat the next day, it is even better.

Keith Knapp
Shakopee, MN

Ramen Noodle Salad

12-oz. bag coleslaw mix

4 green onions, chopped

1 pkg. Ramen noodles, oriental flavor

½ c. toasted almonds, sliced

2 T. sunflower seeds

½ c. oil

2 T. sugar

Ramen noodle seasoning packet

Combine coleslaw mix, onions, noodles, almonds and sunflower seeds. In a separate bowl, mix oil, sugar and seasoning packet. Pour seasoning over coleslaw mix and blend well.

Helene Schroeder
Ponsford, MN

Quick & Easy Vegetable Meat Soup

1 lb. hamburger or ground chuck

2 (15-oz.) cans mixed vegetables

2 (8-oz.) cans tomato sauce

¼ tsp. salt

½ tsp. black pepper

8 oz. water

Cook and drain hamburger. Add remaining ingredients to saucepan. Bring to a boil. Reduce heat and simmer for 20 minutes.

Quinn E. Wood
Cedar Bluff, AL

Buttermilk Biscuits

2 c. flour

1 T. baking powder

¾ tsp. salt

½ tsp. baking soda

5 T. shortening

1 c. buttermilk

In a bowl, mix flour, baking powder, salt and baking soda. Cut in shortening with butter knives or a pastry blender until mixture forms crumbs. Add buttermilk and mix with fork until dough forms. Place dough on floured surface and knead until smooth.

Roll dough to ¾ inch thick. Use a biscuit cutter or a floured glass to cut out biscuits. Place biscuits on ungreased baking sheet. Knead leftover dough and roll out again to make more biscuits. Bake at 425°F for 12 to 15 minutes or until golden brown. Serve hot.

James D. Mullen
East Meredith, NY

Pumpkin Bread

3⅓ c. flour

3 c. sugar

1⅓ tsp. cinnamon

1½ tsp. salt

2 tsp. baking soda

½ tsp. baking powder

1 c. raisins, optional

1 c. canned pumpkin (not the mix)

4 eggs

1 c. oil

⅔ c. water

Mix flour, sugar, cinnamon, salt, baking soda and baking powder. In a separate bowl, mix raisins, pumpkin, eggs, oil and water. Combine flour mixture and pumpkin mixture and pour into 3 1-lb. greased coffee cans. (I spray the cans with nonstick cooking spray.)

Bake for 1 hour at 350°F. When cool, cover with coffee can lids until served.

Henry Schrage
West Sayville, NY

Baked Delicata Squash

1 squash, cut lengthwise, seeds removed

10 ¾-oz. can cream of mushroom soup

Place squash cut side up in 8- to 10-inch square pan. Spoon soup into both halves of squash. Put ¼ inch water in pan. Cover with aluminum foil and bake at 350°F for 45 minutes to 1 hour or until done.

Leonard Zuvela
Everett, WA

Old-Time Zucchini Bread

2 c. baking mix

1½ c. shredded zucchini, lightly packed

¼ c. sugar

½ c. chopped walnuts

¼ c. flour

¼ c. vegetable or olive oil

2 tsp. ground cinnamon

1 tsp. ground nutmeg

1 tsp. vanilla

3 eggs

Preheat oven to 350°F. Grease bottom only of 9 x 5-inch loaf pan. Mix all ingredients and beat vigorously for 30 seconds. Pour into pan and bake for 50 to 55 minutes. Test with wooden toothpick for doneness (toothpick should come out clean when inserted into center of loaf). Cool for 10 minutes. Loosen sides of loaf with knife or spatula and remove by tipping pan over. Wrap cooled bread securely in aluminum foil to store at room temperature for up to 4 days. If desired, wrap securely in aluminum foil, place in plastic bag, seal, label and freeze for up to 1 month.

James Kendrick
Novato, CA

New England Clam Chowder

1 c. shortening

⅓ c. onion, diced

⅓ c. celery, diced

Medium green pepper, diced

1 T. garlic, fresh, minced

1 c. flour

1 gal. fish stock or clam juice, hot

1 lb. 5 oz. (6 to 8) potatoes, peeled and diced

1 qt. clams, canned or frozen

2 tsp. thyme

2 tsp. tarragon

Salt

White pepper

3 qts. milk, hot

Heat shortening in stock pot. Add diced vegetables and garlic; sauté until tender. Add flour, making a roux. Cook for 5 minutes. Add hot stock. Simmer for 5 minutes. Add potatoes, clams and spices. Simmer until potatoes are tender. Add hot milk and stir with wooden spoon. Continue to cook until potatoes are done.

James Mullen
East Meredith, NY

String Beans with Roasted Garlic

1 T. oil

6 cloves garlic, chopped

Dash of salt

Dash of ground pepper

1 lb. fresh string beans, ends cut

Heat oil on medium low. Add garlic, salt and pepper and warm. Add beans. Cook for 4 to 5 minutes, stirring occasionally. Serve hot. Tip: You can use any vegetable for this.

Martha Arango
Bronx, NY

New England Clam Chowder

Greek Salad Dressing

⅓ c. canola oil

3 T. red wine vinegar

1 T. lemon juice

1 T. sugar (optional)

½ tsp. Dijon mustard

Pinch of oregano, to taste

Combine oil, vinegar, lemon juice, sugar, mustard and oregano in a salad dressing-esque container. Shake thoroughly. Chill and serve.

Tip: For a more authentic dressing, use olive oil instead of canola oil if you plan to use the entire batch in one sitting.

Gina Germ
Minneapolis, MN

Greek Salad Dressing

Potato Rolls for Bread Machine

¾ c. lukewarm water

1 egg or 2 egg whites

¾ tsp. salt

⅓ c. sugar

5 T. butter

½ c. mashed potatoes, lukewarm

4 c. bread flour or all-purpose flour

2 tsp. yeast

Place all ingredients in machine in order listed. Program machine for dough and press start. At the end of the cycle, form dough into rolls in ungreased muffin pan.

Bake in preheated 425°F oven for 15 to 18 minutes, or until browned as desired.

Brenda Watts
Nancy, KY

Carole's Marinated Carrots

2 lbs. whole baby carrots, cooked

10¾-oz. can tomato soup

¾ c. sugar

¼ c. vinegar

½ c. salad oil

¼ tsp. mustard

1 green pepper, diced

3 small onions, diced

Combine carrots, soup, sugar, vinegar, oil, mustard, pepper and onions. Chill for at least 24 hours.

Carole Arndt
Roseville, MN

Split Pea Or Lentil Soup

2 c. split peas

Chicken broth, optional

Turkey carcass, ham bone or 2-in. cube salt pork

½ c. chopped onion

1 c. chopped celery with leaves

½ c. chopped carrots

1 clove garlic

1 bay leaf

1 tsp. sugar

Dash of cayenne or 1 pod red pepper

¼ tsp. thyme

2 T. butter or soup fat

2 T. flour

Wash and soak split peas. Drain peas and reserve liquid. Add enough water or chicken broth to reserved liquid to make 10 cups. Add peas again and turkey carcass, ham bone or salt pork. Cover and cook on low for 2½ to 3 hours.

Add onion, celery and carrots; simmer, covered for 30 minutes longer or until tender. Add garlic, bay leaf, sugar, cayenne or red pepper and thyme. Simmer for 10 minutes longer.

Remove bones, carcass or salt pork and bay leaf. Put soup through sieve. Chill. Remove grease. Melt butter. Add flour to butter, stirring until blended. Slowly add a little of the soup mixture. Cook and stir until it boils, then mix it into the rest of the reheated soup. Season to taste.

Sue Davis
Fort Collins, CO

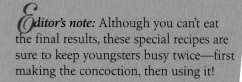

Editor's note: Although you can't eat the final results, these special recipes are sure to keep youngsters busy twice—first making the concoction, then using it!

HUMMINGBIRD MIXTURE

¼ c. sugar
1 c. water
Red food coloring

Mix sugar, water and food coloring and boil for 3 minutes. Let cool before pouring into feeder.

Tip: If you want to steal the hummingbirds from your neighbor's feeder, just add an extra teaspoon of sugar.

FINGER PAINTS

1 envelope unflavored gelatin
½ c. cornstarch
3 T. sugar
Liquid detergent
Food coloring

Soak gelatin in 1/4 cup water. Combine cornstarch and sugar, then gradually add 2 cups water. Cook slowly over low heat, stirring constantly, for about 5 minutes. Remove from heat and add gelatin mixture. Divide into containers and add a drop or two of liquid dish detergent. Last, stir in food coloring.

HOMEMADE BUBBLES

1 part liquid dishwashing detergent
9 parts water
Glycerin

Mix dishwashing detergent with water, adding about ¾ tablespoon glycerin for each cup of the mixture. Reuse wands and containers from store-bought bubbles.

PLAY CLAY

FLOUR-BASED CLAY

1 c. flour
½ c. salt
¼ c. water
½ tsp. vinegar
Food coloring

Mix flour, salt, water and vinegar. Divide into portions and knead food coloring into each.

Store in an airtight container in the refrigerator.

CORNSTARCH-BASED CLAY

1 c. cornstarch
2 c. baking soda
1½ c. water
Food coloring

In a medium-size saucepan, mix cornstarch and baking soda with water until well blended. If you want colored clay, add a few drops of food coloring.

Stir the mixture over medium heat until the clay thickens and forms a ball. Cover with a damp cloth until lukewarm, then knead until smooth and pliable. The clay is now ready to model.

JoAnn Taylor
Fairmont, WV

Hummingbird photo
© Richard Day/Daybreak

Bubbles photo © Erika Stone,
Photo Researchers

Baked Beans a la Camille

2 (21-oz.) cans baked beans

1 small yellow onion, diced very small

1 green pepper, diced very small

½ c. ketchup

¼ c. yellow mustard

½ c. honey

½ c. brown sugar, more or less to taste

1 tsp. red pepper flakes or Tabasco sauce

Put beans, onion, green pepper, ketchup, yellow mustard, honey, brown sugar and red pepper flakes or Tabasco sauce in large pot or slow cooker.

On stove, cook on low heat for about 1 hour; use a "flame-minder" so the beans won't burn. Stir occasionally.

Or, in a slow cooker, cook on low for 2 to 3 hours. This mixture will thicken as it cooks. Adjust seasoning to taste: If it tastes "beany" add a little more brown sugar.

Camille Rafa
Minneapolis, MN

Easy Seasoned Potatoes

4 to 6 medium potatoes, cut into 2" cubes

Olive oil

1 pkg. dry onion soup mix

Place potato cubes in microwaveable dish. Drizzle olive oil over top to coat potatoes. Add soup mix. Microwave on high for 5 minutes. Stir. Microwave for 5 minutes more or until potatoes are tender. Serve.

Russell Koss
Michigan City, IN

Everlasting Salad

20-oz. can pineapple chunks

½ c. sugar

2 T. cornstarch

1 T. lemon juice

⅓ c. orange juice

2 bananas, sliced

15-oz. can peaches or fruit cocktail, drained

Drain pineapple chunks; reserve ¾ cup of pineapple juice. Stir sugar and cornstarch together; add reserved pineapple juice, lemon juice and orange juice. Cook juice mixture, stirring constantly, until thickened, then boil for 1 minute.

While cooked juice mixture is hot, pour over bananas and peaches. Refrigerate salad overnight.

Helene Schroeder
Ponsford, MN

Sweet Yeast Rolls for Bread Machine

Place the following in machine in order listed:

1 c. milk

2 eggs or 3 egg whites, slightly beaten

1 tsp. salt

½ c. sugar

½ c. butter

4½ c. bread flour or all-purpose flour

4½ tsp. yeast

Put machine on dough setting and start. After mixed setting is complete, make into rolls in muffin pan and bake at 350°F for about 15 minutes or until golden brown. Makes 24 rolls.

Brenda Watts
Nancy, KY

Beautiful Soup, Or Hearty Vegetable Beef Soup

Focaccia

Beautiful Soup, Or Hearty Vegetable Beef Soup

½ lb. stewing beef, venison, pork or chicken

Oil for browning meat

15½-oz. can kidney beans

1 small can corn

1 small can green beans

15-oz. can tomato sauce

14½-oz. can stewed tomatoes

½ large onion, chopped

1 c. carrots, cut into small pieces

¾ c. celery, chopped

2 beef bouillon cubes

1 c. chopped cabbage

4 c. water

½ tsp. basil

½ tsp. thyme

¼ tsp. oregano

Salt and pepper to taste

Brown meat in small amount of oil in large pan (Dutch oven works great). Add rest of ingredients. Bring to boil, reduce heat and simmer slowly for at least 1½ to 2 hours. Serve hot, topped with croutons or oyster crackers.

Delicious on a cold day after a hard morning working on a project!

Tip: This soup is easily changed by using leftovers, fresh produce, canned or substitute other vegetables that your family likes (i.e., mushrooms, potatoes, etc.). Each batch tastes different depending on the ingredients, so make it often!

Dale Netherton
Farmington, IA

Focaccia (Italian Flat Bread)

1 pkg. dry yeast

1 c. warm water (105°F)

1 T. sugar

½ tsp. salt

⅓ c. olive oil

3¼ c. flour

In large, warm bowl, sprinkle yeast over warm water. Set aside for 5 minutes to soften. Mix in sugar, salt and oil with wooden spoon. Blend in flour and knead on floured board for 10 minutes or until dough is even and smooth. Place in greased bowl and roll dough around to cover with oil. Cover bowl and let dough rise in warm place for 1 hour.

Punch dough down, knead for 1 minute. Roll out dough to fit a well-greased shallow baking pan. Use knuckles to press deep dimples in dough. Brush olive oil over dough and/or add toppings of choice (see below). Set aside uncovered for 15 minutes. Bake at 450°F for 15 minutes or until brown.

Topping suggestions:
◆ Place sharp cheddar cheese in dimples.
◆ Sprinkle coarse salt and diced onions over top.
◆ Spread a thin layer of pizza sauce over dough and sprinkle with grated Parmesan cheese.

Gary Mallon
Post Falls, ID

CUSTOM-FINISHED PEDESTAL TABLE

This was only my second woodworking project, but my wife and I are enjoying it in its place in our small kitchen. After doing some subtle research, I decided on a style I liked and ordered the single pedestal for the table. I glued up some red oak for the tabletop, using dowel pins to reinforce the joints. When the top was done, I attached it to the pedestal skirt with screws and tabletop fasteners. After several coats of polyurethane (sand between each coat), I decoupaged a pattern onto the top with images I printed off my computer. I also inlaid an eight-section pattern into the top of the table. All in all, I applied 33 coats of finish.

Richard "Cowboy" Solis
Seal Beach, CA

Scalloped Potatoes with Parsley & Cheese

4 medium potatoes

¼ c. onion, minced

½ c. parsley, chopped

8 oz. shredded cheddar cheese

2 T. butter or margarine

1 clove garlic, minced

1½ c. milk

1½ T. cornstarch

Salt and pepper to taste

Parsley, chopped, for garnish

Peel and slice potatoes and arrange half in a well-buttered 2-quart casserole. Top with half the onion, parsley and cheese. Make a second layer of potatoes, onion, parsley and cheese.

Sauté butter and garlic in saucepan for 1 minute or until you smell the garlic. Blend milk, cornstarch, salt and pepper. Pour into pan with garlic and butter; cook and stir until thickened. Pour over potatoes. Bake at 350°F for 1 hour and 15 minutes. Garnish with parsley.

Carole Arndt
Roseville, MN

Bachelor's Baked Potato

Potato

Oil or chicken fat

Salt and pepper

Sour cream

Thoroughly wash and dry a potato. Pierce potato with fork, then cover surface liberally with oil or light fat (chicken fat works great). Set microwave for 1 minute 10 seconds for each inch of potato length (i.e., a 3-inch potato takes 3 minutes 30 seconds). Leave potato in microwave for 1 minute after baking stops. Split potato in half.

Cover liberally with salt, pepper and sour cream. Serve. Needs no additional butter or margarine.

Waldemere Bejnar
Socorro, NM

Street Vendor-Style Onions

3 T. oil

3 to 4 large onions, quartered, then sliced crosswise

1½ T. paprika, preferably sweet

¼ tsp. cumin

¾ tsp. salt

Freshly ground pepper to taste

Water, optional

Heat heavy skillet with oil. Add onions and toss until coated with oil. Add paprika, cumin, salt and pepper. Cover and simmer for 25 minutes or until tender, stirring often. Do not brown. Add a little water if it becomes dry.

William J. Thomas
Ironton, OH

The Ritter Clan's Ancient Family Recipe for Zucchini Bread

⅔ c. shortening

2⅔ c. sugar

4 eggs

1 medium zucchini, grated, not peeled

⅔ c. water

3½ c. flour

2 tsp. baking soda

1½ tsp. salt

½ tsp. baking powder

1 tsp. ground cinnamon

1 tsp. ground cloves

1 lb. fresh blueberries, optional

Heat oven to 350°F. Grease two 9 x 5 x 3-inch or three 8½ x 4½ x 2½-inch loaf pans. In large bowl, cream shortening and sugar until fluffy. Stir in eggs, zucchini and water. Blend in flour, baking soda, salt, baking powder, cinnamon and cloves. Pour into pans and bake for about 70 minutes or until wooden toothpick inserted in center comes out clean.

Tip: If you use self-rising flour, omit baking soda, salt and baking powder. For a real taste treat, add 1 pound fresh blueberries.

Mark Ritter
Salem, OR

Old Settlers' Baked Beans

Mexican Conbread

Old Settlers' Baked Beans

¼ lb. bacon, chopped

1 lb. hamburger

1 medium onion, chopped

⅓ c. brown sugar

⅓ c. white sugar

¼ c. ketchup

¼ c. barbecue sauce

1 tsp. pepper

1 tsp. salt

1 tsp. dry mustard

16-oz. can large red kidney beans

16-oz. can pork and beans

16-oz. can butter beans

Brown bacon, hamburger and onion together. Add sugars, ketchup, barbecue sauce, pepper, salt and dry mustard and mix well. Stir in beans. Bake at 350°F for 1 hour.

Margaret Reed
Portsmouth, OH

Mexican Cornbread

1 c. cornmeal

½ tsp. baking soda

½ tsp. salt

1 c. milk

2 eggs, well beaten

15-oz. can cream-style corn

½ lb. cheese, grated

1 onion, diced

2 to 3 jalapeño peppers, chopped

1 lb. ground meat, browned

In bowl, mix cornmeal, baking soda, salt, milk, eggs and corn. Pour half of batter in ovenproof nonstick skillet. Add cheese, onion, peppers and meat in layers. Top with remaining batter.

Bake at 350°F for 45 to 50 minutes.

Kenneth Slater
Florien, LA

Whiskey Beans
(Drunk Or Bourbon Beans)

¼ c. brown sugar

¼ c. honey

46-oz. can pork and beans

4 to 5 T. Worcestershire sauce

16-oz. bottle chili sauce

½ c. bourbon whiskey

1 large onion, chopped

¼ c. prepared mustard

½ c. green pepper, chopped

Dash of Tabasco sauce, optional

Bacon strips

Preheat oven to 450°F. Combine brown sugar and honey in small bowl. Mix pork and beans, Worcestershire sauce, chili sauce, bourbon, onion, mustard, green pepper and Tabasco sauce in large ovenproof dish. Stir in honey mixture, then top with bacon strips. Bake for about 30 minutes or until bacon is well browned. Flavor is better if prepared the day before serving, then reheated.

Luther Larson
Altoona, IA

Broccoli Salad

1 c. light mayonnaise

½ c. sugar

2 T. vinegar

1 bunch broccoli (3 stalks)

1 small to medium red onion, sliced thin

1 c. roasted sunflower seeds (3.75-oz. bag)

½ c. raisins

6 slices bacon, crisply fried and chopped

Mix mayonnaise, sugar and vinegar in small bowl; set aside. Cut broccoli into bite-size pieces and place in large bowl. Add red onion, sunflower seeds, raisins and bacon. Pour mayo mixture over broccoli mixture and stir well.

Refrigerate for a few hours prior to serving; overnight is better.

Kurt Richter
Gretna, LA

Corn & Black Bean Salad

10-oz. pkg. (about 1½ c.) frozen corn rinsed under cold water and drained

15-oz. can black beans, rinsed and drained

⅓ c. green bell pepper, chopped

4-oz. jar chopped pimientos, drained

¼ c. green onions, chopped (about 6 or 8)

2 T. olive oil

2 T. red wine vinegar

2 T. water

1 to 2 tsp. chili powder

1 tsp. cumin

1 T. sugar

¼ tsp. salt

For salad, combine corn, beans, peppers, pimiento and onions in large bowl. Set aside.

For dressing, mix olive oil, vinegar, water, chili powder, cumin, sugar and salt in small bowl. Pour over salad ingredients and mix well. Chill for at least 2 hours before serving.

Irene O'Brien
Anchorage, AK

Broccoli Salad

Corn & Black Bean Salad

Marinated Carrots

10¾-oz. can tomato soup

¾ c. sugar

1 tsp. dry mustard

½ c. salad oil

¾ c. vinegar

1 tsp. Worcestershire sauce

2 lbs. carrots, sliced and cooked

1 green pepper, sliced thin and small

1 red onion, sliced thin

In large bowl, mix soup, sugar, dry mustard, salad oil, vinegar and Worcestershire sauce. Add carrots, pepper and onion; refrigerate overnight before serving.

Kurt Richter
Gretna, LA

Merri's Zucchini Bread

3 eggs, beaten until light and fluffy

1 c. oil

2 c. sugar

2 c. grated zucchini

3 tsp. vanilla

3 c. flour

1 tsp. salt

1 tsp. soda

3 tsp. cinnamon

¼ tsp. baking powder

1 c. chopped walnuts

1 c. raisins

Mix eggs, oil, sugar, zucchini and vanilla lightly but well. Add flour, salt, soda, cinnamon and baking powder and mix well. Add nuts and raisins. Pour into greased, floured loaf pans and bake for 1 hour at 350°F.

Douglas Fay
Longmont, CO

Nor'-Easterner's Baked Beans

2 (14-oz.) cans navy beans, or 3 cups dried navy beans

½ lb. sliced bacon

1 tsp. salt

1 clove garlic, finely chopped

¼ c. light brown sugar

2 tsp. dry mustard

1 c. dark molasses

1 c. boiling water

If using canned beans, drain.

If you use dried beans, place in a pan and cover with water; let soak overnight, then drain and cover with fresh water and bring to a boil, reduce heat and simmer for 45 minutes. Drain.

Cut bacon into chunks and add to 3-quart casserole dish. Add drained beans and stir until well combined. Mix remaining ingredients except boiling water and pour over beans. Add just enough boiling water to cover the beans. Bake covered for 6 hours and stir once every hour. If beans seem dry after stirring, add some more boiling water. To brown top of beans remove lid for last 30 minutes of cooking.

Kelly Kutz
St. Petersburg, FL

Raisin Broccoli Salad

2 bunches fresh broccoli, cut into small pieces

2 c. raisins

1 c. real mayonnaise (not salad dressing)

1 medium red onion, cut into small pieces

⅓ c. sugar

1 lb. bacon, cooked and crumbled

3 T. sunflower seeds

Mix broccoli, raisins, mayonnaise, onion, sugar and crumbled bacon. Top with sunflower seeds. Best when served cold.

Angela Heltemes
Champlin, MN

BLT Pasta Salad

1 c. mayonnaise or salad dressing

⅓ c. chili sauce

¼ c. lemon juice from concentrate

2 tsp. instant chicken bouillon

2 tsp. sugar

7 oz. elbow macaroni, cooked and drained

1 large tomato, seeded and chopped

¼ c. sliced green onions

4 c. chopped lettuce

8 slices bacon, cooked and crumbled

In large bowl, combine mayonnaise, chili sauce, lemon juice, bouillon and sugar. Stir in macaroni, tomato and onions. Cover and chill. Just before serving, stir in lettuce and bacon. Refrigerate leftovers.

Denise Young
Blaine, MN

ACTIVITY ROOM

I had an open patio attached to the south side of my house. It was not very usable because of the mosquitoes in summer and the cold weather in Fargo. Since I had to reroof the rest of the house, I raised the roof in the project area to match the roofline of the rest of the house. I put two skylights in the roof. I found some windows and a patio door at a garage sale and made the southern view into a sunroom. I insulated it and added an electric baseboard heater. I did the inside in knotty pine tongue-and-groove boards.

We enjoy using the hot tub in winter, when we can watch the snow and cold blowing outside. The room is about 12 ft. x 22 ft. We also use it for an exercise room and to read the morning paper on weekends.

O.J. Weber
Fargo, ND

Party-Time Crab Boil [page 73]

MAIN *dishes*

Whether it's a traditional crab boil, an exotic dish, a downhome casserole or a simple sandwich, the entrée you choose from these pages will nourish and satisfy your family at the dinner table.

Sausage-Stuffed Loaf [page 82]

Smoke House Spaghetti

¼ lb. bacon, cut into small pieces

1 medium onion, chopped

1 lb. ground beef

8-oz. can tomato sauce

1½ tsp. salt

⅛ tsp. pepper

½ tsp. oregano

½ tsp. garlic salt

4-oz. can sliced mushrooms, drained with liquid reserved

8 oz. spaghetti

¼ lb. shredded provolone cheese, divided

Sauté bacon in skillet. Add onion and ground beef. Brown meat mixture. Stir in tomato sauce, salt, pepper, oregano, garlic salt and mushrooms with reserved liquid. Simmer for 15 minutes. Cook spaghetti, drain, stir in sauce. Place half of mixture in buttered 2-quart baking dish. Put half of cheese and then another layer of meat. Add rest of cheese. Bake at 375°F for 20 to 25 minutes or until top is brown and bubbly.

Margaret Reed
Portsmouth, OH

Lemon Chicken

⅓ c. honey

¼ c. lemon juice

2 tsp. crushed rosemary

Chicken breast fillets, skinned

Mix honey, lemon juice and rosemary in shallow dish. Place chicken in marinade and turn after a few minutes. Grill for about 3 minutes on each side. Instead of marinating, you may want to brush the mixture on the chicken as it cooks. If marinated too long the lemon flavor is strong.

Harlan Jache
LaPuente, CA

Petron's Salmon Supreme

10¾-oz. can cream of mushroom soup

1 soup can milk

1 doz. fresh mushrooms, sliced

2 to 3 green onions, cut into ½-inch pieces

2 sprigs parsley, chopped

3 to 4 dashes of black pepper or to taste

4 small or 2 large salmon steaks

Mix soup, milk, mushrooms, onion, parsley and pepper in a bowl. Pour half of mixture into a small baking pan. Lay salmon steaks on top of mixture. Pour remaining mixture on top of steaks. Bake at 325°F for 1 hour or until done. Serve with tossed salad, green peas or asparagus, French bread and French fries.

Leonard Zuvela
Everett, WA

Taco Pinwheels

1½ lbs. hamburger

1½ c. chopped onion

1 pkg. taco seasoning

¼ oz. chives

8-oz. pkg. cream cheese

8 oz. sour cream

1 c. shredded cheddar cheese

5 to 6 flour tortillas

Fry hamburger and onions together. Add taco seasoning and chives. Stir in cream cheese until almost melted. Stir in sour cream. Add cheese. Divide mixture and spread on tortillas, then roll up. Refrigerate. Cut into ½-inch slices. Use taco sauce or salsa for dip.

Raymond Plank
Humboldt, IL

Petron's Salmon Supreme

Speaker Disguise

1

2

3

My wife could not stand having our stereo speakers standing in each corner of our family room. I came up with this idea: I cut a round piece of heavy cardboard (plywood can be used instead), placed it on top of the speaker and secured it with double-faced carpet tape. Then I draped it with cloth that reached to the floor.

This takes on the appearance of a circular table—sturdy enough for a small lamp and accessories. Everyone wonders where the music is coming from and my wife is happy.

William Thomas
Ironton, OH

Barbecued Beef Sandwiches

2 lbs. boned chuck roast

2 c. vertically sliced onion

1 c. bottled barbecue sauce

1 T. cornstarch

1 T. water

Trim fat from roast and cut into 1-inch cubes. Place meat in slow cooker. Stir in the onions and sauce. Cover and cook on low heat for 8 hours.

Remove beef and onions with slotted spoon. Shred beef with 2 forks and set aside. Combine cornstarch and water. Add to barbecue sauce mixture in slow cooker, stirring thoroughly.

Cover with lid and cook on high for 1 minute. Return the shredded beef mixture to slow cooker, cover and cook for 10 minutes more. Serve on rolls.

Leona Matz
Galeton, PA

Rueben Delight

2 to 3 slices corned beef

2 slices Swiss cheese

French bread

Coleslaw

Thousand Island dressing

Place corned beef and cheese on bread. Put coleslaw on top of Swiss cheese. Pour dressing over slaw. Top with other slice of bread.

Todd Fritz
Pittsburgh, PA

Best Potato Casserole

1½ (32-oz.) pkgs. frozen hash brown potatoes

8 oz. sour cream

10¾-oz. can cream of chicken soup

¼ c. chopped onion

2 c. shredded cheddar cheese

Salt

Pepper

1½ c. Corn Flakes, crushed

½ c. butter, melted

Mix potatoes, sour cream, soup, onion, cheese, salt and pepper together. Put into greased 9 x 13-inch pan. Sprinkle Corn Flakes over top. Pour melted butter over crumbs. Bake for 1 hour at 350°F.

Margaret Reed
Portsmouth, OH

Souper Mac 'N' Cheese

7-oz. pkg. elbow macaroni

2 T. margarine, melted, divided

10¾-oz. can condensed cream of mushroom soup

2½ c. shredded sharp cheddar cheese, divided

½ c. sour cream

¼ c. chopped onion

2 slices bread, cubed

Cook macaroni; drain. Toss with 1 tablespoon melted margarine. Add soup, 1 cup cheese, sour cream and onion. Stir well.

Transfer to greased 8-inch-square baking dish. Toss bread cubes with 1 tablespoon melted margarine and sprinkle over casserole. Top with 1½ cups cheese.

Bake uncovered for 30 minutes at 350°F.

Leona Matz
Galeton, PA

Taco Plate

15-oz. can refried beans

16-oz. carton sour cream

1 pkg. taco seasoning

1 jar salsa

8 oz. shredded cheese of your choice

Black olives, chopped

Onions, chopped

Green peppers, chopped

Spread beans on bottom of 9 x 13-inch pan. Mix sour cream and taco seasoning and spread on top of beans. Add a layer of salsa, then sprinkle top with cheese. Top with olives, onions and green peppers as desired. Serve with your favorite tortilla chips.

Mark & Tracia Hogue
White, SD

Fabulously Simple (& Simply Fabulous) Burgers

2 slices dry bread

1 lb. ground beef

2 T. Worcestershire sauce

Salt and pepper

Crumble bread and ground beef into a bowl. Add Worcestershire sauce. Mix well. Form into 4 burgers. Salt and pepper as desired. Grill as desired.

Kevin Frey
Gardner, KS

King Neptune's Chicken

King Neptune's Chicken

6 (8-oz.) chicken breasts

Flour

Egg wash and bread crumbs for breading chicken

Butter for sautéing

4 oz. butter

1 lb. sliced mushrooms

1 bunch scallions, French-cut

4 oz. chopped pimientos

1 lb. sea scallops

2 oz. white wine

8-oz. bottle clam juice

1 tsp. pepper

1 T. lemon pepper

2 c. shrimp stock

2 c. chicken stock

1 c. lobster stock

2 T. cornstarch, mixed with ¼ c. cold water

1 lb. (26 to 30) shrimp, peeled

Cut chicken breasts in half and bread in flour, egg wash and bread crumbs. Melt some butter in a sauté pan and cook breaded chicken until golden brown. Put in pan and set aside.

In a saucepan, melt 4 ounces butter. Add mushrooms, scallions and pimientos and sauté for 1 minute. Add scallops and sauté for 3 minutes. Add wine, clam juice, pepper, lemon pepper and stocks. Add cornstarch mixture and boil until thickened (1 to 2 minutes). Add shrimp after sauce is thick and cook for 3 minutes. Spoon sauce over breaded chicken and serve.

James Mullen
East Meredith, NY

Taco Soup

1 lb. ground beef

1 medium onion, chopped

1 pkg. mild taco seasoning mix

16-oz. can corn

16-oz. can kidney beans, drained and rinsed

28-oz. can stewed tomatoes

8-oz. can tomato sauce

Brown ground beef in heavy saucepan. Drain. Sauté chopped onion; add to ground beef. Stir in taco seasoning, corn, kidney beans, stewed tomatoes and tomato sauce. Simmer for 20 to 30 minutes. Serve topped with tortilla chips, grated cheese and, if desired, a bit of sour cream and some chopped onions.

G. Albert Wimmer
Ogden, UT

Beef Ragoût

6 slices bacon

2½ lbs. sirloin, cut into bite-size pieces

Salt and pepper to taste

14½-oz. can consommé or beef broth

1¼ c. water, divided

½ c. dry red wine or red cooking wine

2 cloves garlic, minced

1 large bay leaf

1 can small pearl onions

18 mini carrots

6 oz. sliced mushrooms

2 T. flour

Fry bacon until crisp and reserve drippings. Crumble bacon and set aside. Brown beef in bacon drippings and pour off excess fat. Add salt and pepper. Add soup and 1 cup water, wine, garlic and bay leaf. Cover and simmer 1½ hours or until beef is tender. Remove bay leaf. Drain onions and add with carrots and mushrooms. Simmer for ½ hour. Blend ¼ cup water with flour and stir into mixture. Add crumbled bacon and serve over cooked noodles or rice.

Darlene Fitzgerld
Grandbury, TX

Carne Vinho e Alhos

(Portuguese marinated meat traditionally served each year on All Kings Day, January 6.)

1 c. cider vinegar

3 T. parsley flakes

¼ tsp. black pepper

1 tsp. salt

¼ to ½ tsp. thyme

10 cloves garlic, quartered

8 oz. vermouth cooking wine

7 to 8 lb. Boston butt; pork blade meat can be used

Paprika as needed

9 bay leaves

6 (15-oz.) cans small white whole potatoes, drained

1 loaf Portuguese bread, cut into 1-in. slices

Mix vinegar, parsley, pepper, salt, thyme, garlic and vermouth in a medium nonaluminum mixing bowl. Debone meat, cut into 2-inch cubes and place on wax paper. Sprinkle meat with paprika, turning to season both sides. Soak meat in vinegar marinade, then place in glass or stainless bowl in layers. Place several whole bay leaves in between layers. Pour any leftover wine on top of meat and place on bottom shelf of refrigerator for 2 days.

Rotate meat once in the morning and once at night (i.e., top to bottom, etc.). Place meat and marinade in a large pan. Cook on medium heat for 1¼ hours on top of stove. Place potatoes in a large roasting pan and mix in the cooked meat. Use only some of the marinade on the potatoes.

Bake on center rack at 375°F for 20 minutes. Remove from oven and slightly dip sliced bread into marinade, then place wet side face up on top of meat and potatoes mixture. Return pan to oven and broil until bread starts to toast. Remove and serve with applesauce, 3-bean salad and a glass of wine. Enjoy!

Vern & Rose Pereira
Cumberland, RI

Tom's Italian Sausage, Peppers & Onions

Olive oil

2 lbs. sweet Italian sausage

2 lbs. hot Italian sausage

4 large sweet red bell peppers, sliced lengthwise

4 large sweet yellow peppers

Large white onion, cut lengthwise

Small clove garlic, cut lengthwise

Salt and pepper

1 c. crushed tomatoes

1 to 2 c. red wine

Cooked pasta of your choice

Heat olive oil in large pan or slow cooker. Place sausage in pan and cook until done. Slice sausages 1 inch thick; return to pan.

Add peppers. When peppers are soft, add onion, garlic, salt and pepper. Bring all to a simmer. Add tomatoes and wine slowly. Cook for 10 minutes.

Remove all food from sauce and save liquid; do not strain. Add salt and pepper to taste. Place sausage on pasta. Pour juices over sausage.

Tom Cane
Norristown, PA

Nadine's February Chili

1 medium onion, chopped

3 to 4 cloves garlic, minced

½ c. chopped celery

½ c. chopped green pepper

1 lb. lean ground beef, browned and drained

6-oz. can tomato paste

½ tsp. ground cumin

⅛ tsp. black pepper

2 T. chili powder

⅛ to ¼ tsp. Tabasco sauce

1 tsp. oregano

1 T. parsley flakes

1 to 2 T. sugar

Pinch of cayenne pepper

1 bay leaf

1 T. Worcestershire sauce

14-oz. can beef broth

4-oz. can sliced mushrooms

15-oz. can chopped or diced tomatoes

4½-oz. can green chiles

½ of 16-oz. can black olives, chopped

15-oz. can light red kidney beans

16-oz. can baked beans

Sour cream

Finely shredded cheddar cheese

Diced onion, optional

Sauté onion, garlic, celery, and green pepper in Dutch oven. Add ground beef and mix well. Stir in tomato paste. Mix in seasonings. Add broth, then mushrooms, tomatoes, chiles, black olives and beans. Stir well.

Simmer for about 1 hour. Top with sour cream, finely shredded cheddar cheese and diced onion. Serve with crackers or white tortilla chips.

Jack Trimble
Fremont, IN

INSECT TRAP

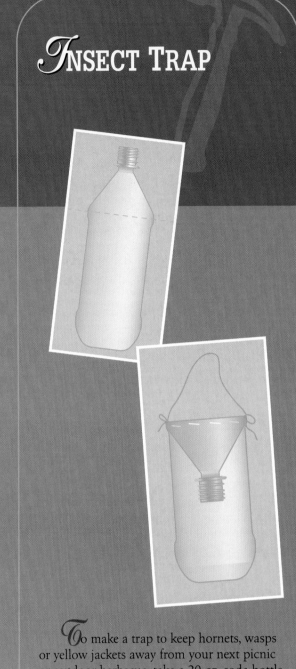

To make a trap to keep hornets, wasps or yellow jackets away from your next picnic or outdoor barbecue, take a 20-oz. soda bottle and cut off the top just below the neck. Invert the top and set it inside the bottom section. Staple around the joint. You can staple a string to the edge to form a hanging loop.

Place a small amount of liquid like sweet soda or hummingbird food inside the bottle. When the trap is full of flying insects fill it with water and discard it.

Kenneth Slater
Florien, LA

Mexican Pizza

2 (8-oz.) pkgs. refrigerated crescent rolls

8-oz. pkg. cream cheese, softened

8 oz. sour cream

1 lb. ground beef

1 envelope taco seasoning mix

2¼ oz. sliced black olives, drained

1 medium tomato, chopped

¾ c. shredded mozzarella cheese

¾ c. shredded cheddar cheese

1 c. shredded lettuce

Unroll crescent roll dough and place in ungreased 15 x 10 x 1-inch baking pan. Flatten dough to fit the pan, sealing seams and perforations. Bake at 375°F for 8 to 10 minutes or until light golden brown; cool. In a small bowl, blend cream cheese and sour cream with wire whisk; spread over crust. Chill for 30 minutes.

Meanwhile, brown beef in a skillet; drain; stir in taco seasoning. Add water according to taco seasoning package and simmer for 5 minutes, stirring occasionally. Spread over cream cheese layer. Top with olives, tomatoes, cheese and lettuce. Cut into serving-size pieces. Serve immediately or refrigerate.

Sharon Matheny
Van Wert, OH

Best Ribs In Town

8 lbs. baby back ribs

½ c. white vinegar

2 c. water

Barbecue sauce

Season ribs with pepper and garlic powder. Place in roaster with vinegar and water; bake at 250°F for 2 hours. Remove ribs from pan and place on grill long enough to brown on each side, adding barbecue sauce while on grill. Return ribs to clean roaster and bake at 250°F for 1 hour or until ready to serve. Add more sauce if desired. Serve with Easy Seasoned Potatoes (see page 45).

Russell Koss
Michigan City, IN

Slow-Cooker Lasagna

1 lb. ground round

1 tsp. Italian seasoning

28-oz. jar spaghetti sauce

⅓ c. water

8 uncooked lasagna noodles

15 oz. ricotta cheese or cottage cheese

2 c. mozzarella cheese, divided

Cook beef with seasoning. Add spaghetti sauce and water. Lightly grease 5-quart cooker and put 4 uncooked lasagna noodles in bottom. Layer with half of beef and sauce mixture. Add all of ricotta or cottage cheese. Add 1 cup mozzarella cheese. Layer with rest of noodles, meat sauce mix and mozzarella cheese. Cook on high for 1 hour or on low for 5 hours.

Tim & Tammy Kriesel
Russellville, AR

Fish Tacos

White fish (northern cod)

1 c. flour, seasoned with garlic powder and pepper

1 c. beer

½ c. mayonnaise

½ c. plain yogurt

Canola oil

Soft corn tortillas

Shredded cabbage

Salsa

Lime juice

Wash fish in cold, lightly salted water or water with a bit of lemon juice. Drain on paper towels. Fish should be dry before dipping in batter.

While fish is drying, combine flour, garlic powder and pepper; add beer to flour mixture.

In a separate bowl, mix mayonnaise and yogurt; refrigerate until fish is ready to eat.

When fish is dry, dip in batter and fry in canola oil until it flakes easily with fork.

Place fish in warm soft corn tortilla. Top with mayo-yogurt sauce, shredded cabbage, salsa and lime juice.

Margaret Tchida
St. Cloud, MN

Lewis's Hamburger Noodle Casserole

8 oz. wide or extra wide egg noodles

1 to 1½ lbs. lean ground beef

1 onion, chopped

2 cloves garlic, crushed, or 2 T. minced dry garlic

Pepper to taste

3 (8-oz.) cans tomato sauce

8 oz. shredded cheese

Cook noodles according to package directions until almost done. Brown ground beef, then add onion, garlic and pepper. Cook until onions are almost tender. Add tomato sauce; heat until bubbly. In 2-quart baking dish, put ground beef mixture, top with noodles. Then sprinkle cheese on top to cover noodles completely. Bake at 350°F for 30 to 35 minutes or until cheese is melted and starting to brown.

Recipe can be doubled or tripled. You can use your favorite sloppy joe mixture in place of this hamburger mixture, but don't use a thick mixture.

Lewis Newell
Cassopolis, MI

Dani's Cornish Hens

4 T. butter

2 half-full cans beer

1 onion, sliced

Garlic, sliced

Dash of salt and pepper

Parsley

2 Cornish hens

Slice butter into 4 equal pieces. Place 2 of the pieces of butter into each half-can of beer. Add slices of onion, garlic, salt, pepper and parsley. Insert can of beer into the cavity of the hen so that the can is standing up with the hen on top. Place beer can on grill. Grill for 1½ to 2 hours or until juices run clear. Guaranteed delicious because it cooks from inside out.

Steven Carroll
Franklin, MA

Greek Pizza

¾ c. sour cream

3 tsp. fresh basil, chopped

Pizza crust (your choice)

1½ c. chopped fresh spinach

3 Roma tomatoes, sliced

20 Greek olives, sliced

6½ oz. artichoke hearts

¾ c. crumbled feta cheese

Mix sour cream and basil; spread on crust. Arrange toppings in circular rings with spinach in outer ring, then tomatoes, olives and artichokes on inside. Sprinkle cheese over entire pizza. Bake at 425°F for 18 to 20 minutes.

Julie Carpenter
Plymouth, MN

Chili

1 medium onion, chopped

3 cloves garlic, minced

2 (15½-oz.) cans chili beans

28 oz. red chili sauce, medium hot

4-oz. can diced green chiles

1 tsp. oregano

28-oz. can diced tomatoes

6-oz. can tomato paste

1 tsp. salt

1 tsp. cumin

2 c. powdered mashed potatoes

Sauté onion and garlic in large pan sprayed with non-stick spray. Add beans, chili sauce, chiles, oregano, tomatoes, tomato paste, salt and cumin and cook for 6 hours on low heat in slow cooker. To thicken, add powdered mashed potatoes.

Harlan Jache
LaPuente, CA

Greek Pizza

Apple Pancake Or Oven French Toast

2 large apples

8 1-inch-thick slices of large French bread

5 T. butter

1 c. dark brown sugar

2 T. dark corn syrup

1 tsp. ground cinnamon

3 large eggs

1 c. milk

1 tsp. vanilla

Day 1: Peel, core and slice apples; toast French bread. Melt butter over medium heat, add apples and cook until tender. Add sugar, corn syrup and cinnamon; stir until sugar dissolves. Pour apple mixture into 9 x 13-inch pan, then arrange toast over top of apples.

In medium bowl, beat eggs, milk and vanilla until well blended. Pour over apple toast mixture. Refrigerate overnight.

Day 2: Bake at 375°F for 30 to 35 minutes or until firm. Turn out apple side up and serve.

Kelly Kutz
St. Petersburg, FL

Barbecued Beef Short Ribs

3 to 4 lbs. beef short ribs

Favorite barbecue sauce

Allow a few pounds of ribs to warm to room temperature for about an hour. Then completely cover them with your favorite bottled barbecue sauce. Place ribs on medium hot flame on barbecue grill. Turn every 15 minutes. Baste with more sauce each time you turn them. Continue cooking and turning for 2 to 3 hours depending on how well done you want them. The sauce will glaze to a thick, chewy flavorful layer on the outside.

Kelly Kutz
St. Petersburg, FL

Slow-Cooked Meatloaf Dinner

2 lbs. hamburger

2 packs saltine crackers, crushed

4 eggs

½ c. barbecue sauce

2 pkgs. dried onion soup mix

1 medium onion, finely chopped

4-oz. can chopped mushrooms, drained

1 T. dry Italian seasoning

4 medium potatoes, cut into chunks

2 (14½-oz.) cans green beans

Mix hamburger, cracker crumbs, eggs, barbecue sauce, soup mix, onion, mushrooms and Italian seasoning in a large bowl. Shape into loaf. Place in slow cooker. Put half of potatoes on each side of loaf. Put one can of beans on each side of loaf, making sure liquid from beans covers potatoes. Add water if potatoes are not covered so potatoes don't get brown and gummy.

Cover slow cooker and set in refrigerator overnight. Remove from refrigerator in the morning. Keep lid on pot and set on low to cook for 8 to 12 hours.

Leroy Turner
New Pairs, PA

Pork Hock Stew

3 c. water

1 large onion

1 lb. cut-up fresh pork hock

1 tsp. salt

1 T. parsley flakes

10¾-oz. can cream of mushroom soup

2 medium potatoes, cubed

Peas, optional

Put water, onion, pork, salt and parsley in pan. Bring to a boil. Turn down heat and simmer a couple of hours or until meat is tender. Add soup and potatoes and cook on medium heat until potatoes are done. Add peas and cook for an additional 5 minutes. Serve hot.

Roy W. Personius
Carthage, MO

REFURBISHED POOL TABLE

$\mathcal{M}$y father purchased a pool table he had played on when he was a teenager in the era when pool halls were the "hang-out." This table is now 130 years old and was built in Syracuse, NY.

When it was given to me it was in great disrepair. The frame had been dismantled to move it into my brother's basement, where it had sat unassembled for about 10 years. It had been painted deck brown, so I resurfaced it totally.

This project took me all of one winter to complete. This was the first pool table that I have ever reconditioned. With guidance from a local pool table refinishing business I tackled the job.

Tony Indilicato
Altamont, NY

Party-Time Crab Boil

Party-Time Crab Boil

2 cloves garlic, crushed

2 (1½-oz.) pkgs. crab or shrimp boil

Salt and pepper to taste

10 whole potatoes with skins

5 ears sweet corn on the cob, broken into halves

2 links mild Italian sausage, cut into 2½-inch pieces

2 lbs. crab legs, defrosted

3 lbs. shrimp, defrosted

Fill 16-quart stock pot about half full with water; bring to a boil. Add garlic and seasoning from seafood boil packages; boil for 5 minutes. Add salt and pepper and potatoes; boil for 5 minutes. Add corn and sausage; boil for 10 minutes.

Add crab legs; boil for 5 minutes. Add shrimp; boil for 5 minutes. Add water as necessary.

If crab pliers are unavailable, slide one tine of a stout fork into a crab leg at the joint and lever up to split the leg. Don a waterproof bib with spill pocket at the bottom and enjoy!

Thomas Thurber
Myrtlewood, AL

Blondie's Secret Catfish Batter

2 (8½-oz.) pkgs. cornmeal mix

2 small pkgs. biscuit mix

2 eggs

1½ tsp. garlic powder

2½ tsp. seasoning salt

½ tsp. black pepper

1 tsp. onion salt

½ tsp. poultry seasoning

2 pinches of parsley

12-oz. can beer

Catfish (or fish of choice), deboned, filleted and cut into 1 or 1½-inch squares (very important)

Mix cornmeal mix, biscuit mix, eggs, garlic, seasoning salt, pepper, onion salt, poultry seasoning and parsley. Slowly stir in beer until you have a thin but not runny batter.

Dip pieces of fish into batter and drop into hot oil until golden brown, then drop into bowl lined with paper towels.

Batter is good for any fish and also spring mushrooms. Remaining batter can be used to make hush puppies by adding a little cornmeal until batter is fairly thick. Just drop by teaspoon into hot oil.

Sherry Harvey
Sparks, OK

Shrimp Etouffée

1 large onion, chopped

2 cloves garlic, chopped

½ bell pepper, chopped

½ c. butter or margarine

10¾-oz. can cream of mushroom soup

14½-oz. can diced tomatoes

1 lb. shrimp

Sauté onions, garlic and bell pepper in butter. Add soup and tomatoes. Bring to a boil, stirring constantly. Lower heat and add shrimp. Cover and simmer for 20 to 25 minutes, stirring as needed to prevent sticking. Season to taste, preferably with Cajun seasoning. Serve over rice.

Shawn O'Quinn
Jennings, LA

West Coast BLT

1 lb. bacon

6 croissants, warmed if desired

½ c. mayonnaise

¼ c. Thousand Island dressing

6 lettuce leaves

Chicken breast luncheon meat, sliced

2 tomatoes, sliced

2 California avocados, seeded, peeled and sliced

Fry bacon until crisp; drain and set aside. Split each croissant in half lengthwise. Mix mayonnaise and dressing in small bowl. Spread each cut side of croissant with mayonnaise mixture. On bottom croissant half, layer 1 leaf of lettuce, 1 slice of chicken, 2 tomato slices, 2 strips bacon and 4 avocado slices. Replace croissant top.

Donna Miller
Collierville, TN

Ham & Cheese Delights

½ c. chopped onion

1 T. butter

2 c. finely chopped ham

3 eggs, beaten

1 c. American cheese

⅔ c. crushed crackers

1½ c. milk

Cook onion. Add butter, ham, eggs, cheese, crackers and milk. Put into 6 x 10-inch dish. Bake at 350°F for 40 to 45 minutes.

Sharon Matheny
Van Wert, OH

Beef & Shrimp in Dijonaise Mushroom Sauce

10 oz. (1-oz. cubes) butter

1 lb. 4 oz. cubed beef tips

1 lb. (31 to 35) shrimp

1 lb. sliced mushrooms

10 oz. beef broth

1 bunch green onions, chopped

5 T. Dijon mustard

Salt and pepper to taste

3 tsp. parsley

Melt 5 ounces butter in sauté pan. Add beef and shrimp. Cook for about 4 to 5 minutes. Add mushrooms and cook for 2 minutes. Add beef broth, green onions, mustard, salt, pepper and parsley. Cook for 5 minutes. Add remaining 5 ounces butter over low heat. Serve over hot noodles or rice.

James Mullen
East Meredith, NY

Pork Fried Rice
(3-generation family recipe)

2½ to 3-lb. Boston butt (pork shoulder roast), cubed into 1-in. chunks

1 large onion, diced

½ c. soy sauce, divided

Cayenne pepper

10 eggs

Salt and pepper

6 to 8 servings instant rice

15-oz.can bean sprouts, drained

Salt and pepper to taste

Brown pork in large frying pan. Add onion, ¼ cup soy sauce and 4 to 5 shakes cayenne pepper. Simmer for 1 to 1½ hours, stirring occasionally. Break eggs into bowl, add ¼ cup soy sauce and 4 to 5 shakes cayenne pepper. Season with salt and pepper as with any scrambled eggs. Beat eggs and seasonings, then scramble them in large frying pan. Prepare rice according to package directions. Mix pork, onion, scrambled eggs, rice and sprouts to one large frying pan and mix and fry for 5 minutes.

Pack fried rice into cereal bowl and turn upside down onto plate to form a nice mound. Season to taste with additional soy sauce, salt and pepper. Serve with buttered soda crackers and beverage of your choice.

Steve Warner
Norfolk, NE

Tom's It's-So-Good-It's-Disgusting Chicken

3 to 4 lbs. chicken pieces (legs, thighs, breasts or wings)

Barbecue sauce

Salt and pepper

Boil chicken in 3 to 4 quarts water. Don't put too much chicken in pot. Boil until chicken is fully cooked, about 10 minutes.

Carefully remove chicken from pot and drain dry. Set broth aside. Spread layer of barbecue sauce evenly in large pan. Layer chicken in pan. Do not pile up. Spread sauce over chicken. Put pan on grill over medium heat.

Let chicken cook in sauce until it begins to fall off bones. Continue cooking. If sauce gets too thick, add some reserved broth. If you need more than one layer of chicken, wait until first pan is done, then prepare a second pan. Salt and pepper to taste.

Tom Cane
Norristown, PA

Fish-Fry Batter

1 c. pancake mix

1 tsp. salt

1 12-oz. can beer

Combine pancake mix and salt. Add beer; stir batter. Dry fish on paper towel and dip into batter before frying.

Margaret Reed
Portsmouth, OH

1948 Original Barbecue Sauce

1 medium onion, chopped

2 cloves garlic, minced

2 T. butter, melted

14-oz. can whole tomatoes

½ c. celery, finely chopped

⅓ c. vinegar

¼ c. green pepper, finely chopped

2 fresh celery leaves, finely chopped

1 bay leaf

3 T. molasses

1½ tsp. salt

2 tsp. dry mustard

2 tsp. hot sauce

½ tsp. ground cloves

½ tsp. ground allspice

2 lemon slices

Sauté onion and garlic in butter in a saucepan until clear. Stir in remaining ingredients. Bring to a boil. Reduce heat and simmer uncovered for 30 minutes, stirring occasionally.

Discard bay leaf and lemon slices. Process mixture in a food mill if you desire a smoother sauce.

This is recommended for chicken, but if you leave out celery ingredients, it makes a good sauce for just about anything.

Kelly Kutz
St. Petersburg, FL

Perfect Italian Hoagie

Hard hoagie bun or Italian bread loaf, sliced

Golden Italian dressing

Ham

Capicola

Hard Salami

Pepperoni

Provolone cheese

Lettuce, shredded

Salt and pepper

Vinegar and oil

Tomato slices

Red onion slices

Place split hoagie bun on baking sheet; pour dressing on bun. Top with ham, capicola, salami and pepperoni. Bake at 350°F until bun starts to brown. Add a few slices of cheese until it melts. Remove from oven and add lettuce, salt, pepper, vinegar and oil to your liking. Add tomato and onion slices.

Todd Fritz
Pittsburgh, PA

Grilled Cordon Bleu Sandwich

Chicken breast

3 slices bacon

Kaiser bun

2 slices ham luncheon meat

2 slices Swiss cheese

Grill chicken breast. Cook bacon. Place chicken on bun and top with ham, Swiss cheese and bacon.

Todd Fritz
Pittsburgh, PA

Perfect Italian Hoagie

Grilled Cordon Bleu Sandwich

BASEMENT REMODEL

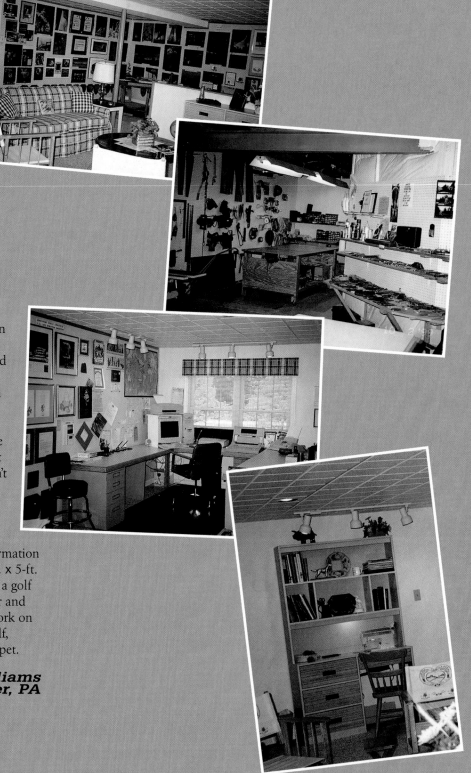

The walk-out basement in my house gave me the opportunity to make an office/work area, plus a sewing area for my wife and a sitting/sofa-bed area for guests. I added a bathroom just to have one on this level.

The walls are homosote wallboard covered with felt so the push pin marks won't show when removed. The wood shop area is large enough for all of the projects I make (for example, a 4-ft. x 4-ft. x 6-ft.-tall information kiosk for my church, a 4-ft. x 5-ft. brochure display unit, and a golf club stand for my daughter and son-in-law). I did all the work on the basement project myself, except I did not lay the carpet.

***Lawrence Williams
West Chester, PA***

Spaghetti Pie

½ lb. ground beef

1 lb. sausage

½ c. chopped onion

1 clove garlic, minced

15-oz. can tomato sauce

6-oz. can tomato paste

1 tsp. basil

1 tsp. oregano

6 oz. thin spaghetti

¼ c. butter

½ c. grated Parmesan cheese

1 large egg, beaten

1 c. ricotta cheese

8 oz. mozzarella cheese, shredded

Sauté beef, sausage, onion and garlic in skillet over medium heat until meat is cooked. Add tomato sauce and paste, basil and oregano. Simmer for 30 minutes. Meanwhile, cook spaghetti according to package directions.

Drain spaghetti and chop into pieces. Combine spaghetti with butter, Parmesan cheese and egg; press mixture into bottom of 12-inch pie plate. Spread with ricotta, then meat, then mozzarella cheese. Bake for 30 minutes at 350°F.

Steven Carroll
Franklin, MA

Quick & Easy Swedish Meatballs

MEATBALLS:

1 lb. ground turkey or lean ground beef

1½ c. plain bread crumbs

⅓ tsp. nutmeg

½ tsp. black pepper

1 egg

1 tsp. Worcestershire sauce

Mix ground meat, bread crumbs, nutmeg, pepper, egg and Worcestershire sauce in large bowl. Form into meatballs. Place on baking sheet sprayed with vegetable cooking spray. Bake at 400°F for 8 to 10 minutes. Turn meatballs over and bake for another 8 to 10 minutes.

SAUCE:

1 envelope onion soup mix

1½ c. water

¼ c. white vinegar

2 T. sugar

3 T. cornstarch dissolved in ¾ c. cold water

½ of 20-oz. can pineapple tidbits

In large skillet, over medium heat, combine soup mix, water, vinegar and sugar. Bring to a simmer. Stir in cornstarch mixture and pineapple. Add cooked meatballs. Simmer for 5 minutes. Serve over hot, cooked noodles.

Irene O'Brien
Anchorage, AK

Pineapple-Teriyaki Pork Chops
& Grilled Portabella Mushrooms

Pineapple-Teriyaki Pork Chops & Grilled Portabella Mushrooms

1 to 2 (6-oz.) cans unsweetened pineapple juice

2 to 3 tsp. sugar

2 to 4 T. teriyaki sauce

1 pork loin, sliced into chops about ½ inch thick

Garlic powder

Salt and pepper

3 to 4 whole portabella mushroom caps

8-oz. bottle balsamic vinegar and herb salad dressing

Mix pineapple juice, sugar and teriyaki sauce in a shallow casserole dish, stirring until sugar dissolves. Using a fork, poke several holes in each side of the chops (but not all the way through). Marinate for 2 to 3 hours in refrigerator turning several times. Sprinkle chops with garlic, salt and pepper to taste and put on a gas grill over low flame (sugar burns easily) or cook indirectly over charcoal, turning and brushing with marinade several times until done.

Wash and lightly scrub mushrooms under cool running water and pat dry with paper towels. Slice into fairly thick slices and put in 1 gallon zip-top storage bag; shake dressing well and pour over mushrooms. Seal bag. Place flat on refrigerator shelf for 2 to 3 hours, turning several times. Grill over very low heat, turning several times until tender and done.

Mike Miller
Richmond, VA

Italian Meatloaf

2 lbs. hamburger

2 c. bread crumbs

¼ c. Parmesan cheese

2 eggs

Dash of salt and pepper

15-oz. can or jar tomato sauce (your favorite), divided

8-oz. pkg. shredded cheese

8 slices bacon, cooked, optional

Combine hamburger, bread crumbs, Parmesan cheese, eggs, salt, pepper, half jar tomato sauce and a handful of shredded cheese. Place into meatloaf pans. Place bacon on top of uncooked meatloaf. Bake at 350°F for 30 minutes. Remove from oven and drain excess grease. Spread remaining sauce and cheese on top. Return to oven for 30 more minutes. Tip: If meatloaf mixture is dry, add more sauce. If it's too wet, add more bread crumbs.

Steven Carroll
Franklin, MA

Grilled Caesar Chicken

10 to 12 boneless, skinless chicken breasts, thinly sliced

5 to 6 cloves garlic, crushed

16-oz. bottle Caesar salad dressing

Marinate the chicken with garlic and dressing in glass bowl in refrigerator for at least 2 hours or as long as overnight. Remove chicken from marinade and discard mixture. Cook chicken as desired.

Katie & Julie Tapper
Philadelphia, PA

Sausage-Stuffed Loaf

2 Italian sausages

½ lb. ground beef

½ c. chopped onion

¼ c. chopped green pepper

1 medium tomato, chopped

15-oz. can chunky Italian tomato sauce

½ tsp. dried basil

½ tsp. sugar

¼ tsp. anise seed

¼ tsp. salt

⅛ tsp. garlic powder

1 loaf French bread

¼ c. Parmesan cheese, shredded

Cook sausage in skillet until no longer pink. Remove and set aside. In same skillet, cook beef, onion and green pepper; drain. Stir in tomato, tomato sauce and seasonings. Cut sausages in half lengthwise and slice; add to meat sauce.

Cut a wedge out of top of bread about 2 inches wide and three-fourths of the way through bread. Fill bread with meat sauce; sprinkle with cheese.

Wrap in foil and bake at 400°F for 15 to 20 minutes. Great for football games, picnics and other informal gatherings.

Bart Christy
Ijamsville, MD

Sausage-Stuffed Loaf

BACKYARD GET-AWAY

My wife and I enjoy sitting around a campfire and cooking casual meals. However, we prefer not to travel. So we decided to build our own campfire site in our backyard. We pictured a campfire site with a privacy lattice.

Our first thoughts were the materials. We purchased sand, pea gravel, large, round stepping-stones, a used truck tire rim and a shovel and a rack. We made our area about 8 feet in diameter. We dug a hole in the center about 1 foot deep and 3 feet in diameter and filled it about half full of pea gravel. Then we put a truck tire rim in the center of the hole so about 3 inches of the tire rim was above ground. After things looked centered we filled the inside and the outside of the rim up to ground level with pea gravel. About 4 inches away from the pea gravel and the tire rim, we placed decorative patio bricks to form an outer circle to keep the fire contained. Last of all, we smoothed the outer area around the pit, added fine sand and laid 8 large round patio stepping-stones, spaced evenly.

To make the privacy background, we set four 4 x 6 posts to support lattice panels and an overhead arbor made with 2 x 10 joists and 2 x 6 crosspieces. We added the wood stacks for more privacy and to make firewood readily available whenever we decided to have an evening around the campfire.

It has been quite a rewarding project for both of us.

We call it: The Backyard Get-Away.

Roger & Lynn Pletcher
Elkhart, IN

Scott's Killer Meatloaf

3 slices bread

3 lbs. ground round or ground chuck

3 eggs

¼ c. milk

¼ medium onion, diced

Ginger

Cinnamon

Onion salt to taste (as much as the regular salt)

Garlic salt, generous amount

Nutmeg

Sage, minimal amount

Rosemary

Thyme

Cloves

Salt to taste

Pepper to taste

6 oz. hot picante sauce (reduce to 4½ oz. if that's too spicy)

Preheat oven to 300°F. Tear bread slices into ¼-inch cubes (tear by hand; it will taste different if cubes are larger or cut with knife). Combine all ingredients in a large bowl. Mix thoroughly, squeezing everything through your fingers until you have one large thoroughly mixed ball with no free liquid.

Place meat mixture in 9 x 13-inch pan and shape. Cover and bake for 1 hour. Pour off liquid and reduce temperature to 250°F. Uncover and finish baking for 2½ hours. Leftovers make great sandwiches.

Scott Cloyd
Pierce City, MO

Crawfish Fettuccine

1 large onion, chopped

½ bell pepper, chopped

2 cloves garlic, chopped

½ c. butter or margarine

10-oz. can cream of mushroom soup

8 to 16 oz. Velveeta Jalapeño Cheese, cut into small cubes

16-oz pkg. fettuccine

1 lb. crawfish or shrimp

Cajun seasoning

Sauté onions, pepper and garlic in butter until soft. Add soup and cheese. Lower heat to a simmer. Prepare noodles according to package directions. Add shrimp and season with some form of Cajun seasoning to taste. Cook just until shrimp turn pink. Add fettuccine and mix well. Serve with green salad and garlic bread stuffed with mozzarella cheese.

Shawn O'Quinn
Jennings, LA

Kentucky-Style Sauce

1¾ c. water

1 c. plus 2 T. ketchup

¼ c. plus 2 T. Worcestershire sauce

1½ tsp. red pepper

1 tsp. paprika

1 tsp. dry mustard

¾ tsp. garlic salt

¾ tsp. onion powder

¾ tsp. black pepper

Stir together water, ketchup, Worcestershire sauce, red pepper, paprika, dry mustard, garlic salt, onion powder and black pepper; simmer over medium heat for 20 minutes. Best on chicken or ribs.

Kelly Kutz
St. Petersburg, FL

Cajun Surf & Turf Tips

3½ lbs. (31 to 35) shrimp, peeled

1 lb. butter (1-oz. cubes), divided

3½ lbs. cubed beef

½ T. salt

1 tsp. cayenne pepper

½ tsp. white pepper

½ tsp. black pepper

1 tsp. crushed basil

1 tsp. crushed thyme

1 tsp. crushed oregano

6 c. sliced mushrooms

2½ c. chopped green onion

1 c. shrimp stock

¼ c. chicken stock

Peel shrimp and boil shells for shrimp stock. In large sauté pan, combine 10 ounces cubed butter, cubed beef, salt, peppers, basil, thyme and oregano; sauté until meat is well browned. Add shrimp, mushrooms and green onion; sauté for about 5 minutes. Add shrimp stock and chicken stock. Simmer until reduced and slightly thickened. Add remaining 6 ounces butter over low heat.

James Mullen
East Meredith, NY

Glen's Goulash Barbecue Style

1 lb. lean ground beef

Salad oil, optional

¾ lb. mushrooms, sliced

2 medium onions, chopped

1 medium green bell pepper, stemmed, seeded and chopped

1 tsp. dry oregano leaves or Italian spices

8 oz. spaghetti noodles

1¼ c. barbecue sauce

Fresh parsley, chopped, optional

Grated Parmesan cheese, optional

In a 6-quart pan, cook beef over medium heat until browned and crumbly, about 15 minutes. Add oil if needed; discard all but 2 tablespoons fat. Add mushrooms, onions, green pepper and spices; stir often until onion is soft, about 10 minutes. Meanwhile, fill another 6-quart pan two-thirds full with water; bring to a boil. Add spaghetti and boil uncovered until tender, about 10 to 12 minutes. Drain pasta well and add to beef mixture along with barbecue sauce. Stir and cook until hot. Pour onto a platter and top with parsley or Parmesan cheese.

Glen Fulcher
Seattle, WA

Cajun Surf & Turf Tips

Chicken à la Fay

4 to 6 chicken breasts, cut up and fried

2 (6-oz.) pkgs. Spanish rice

2 (16-oz.) jars green chile salsa

2 c. shredded sharp cheddar cheese

Place chicken, rice, salsa and cheese in slow cooker or large saucepan.

Options according to individual taste:

Tomato paste

Corn tortillas, shredded

Mexi-style corn

Hominy

Jalapeños

A very fun and flexible dish with lots of room for creativity. Try varying the ingredient amounts or adding your own.

Douglas Fay
Longmont, CO

Ground Beef Stroganoff

½ c. chopped onion

Minced garlic, to taste

½ c. margarine or butter

1 lb. ground beef

½ tsp. salt

¼ tsp. pepper

1 T. flour

10¾-oz. can cream of mushroom soup

1 c. sour cream

Dill weed to taste, optional

Sauté onions and garlic in margarine. Add beef, salt and pepper. Stir until all pieces are cooked. Sprinkle flour over top. Add soup and sour cream. Cook over low heat. Mix well. Serve over cooked noodles. Sprinkle with dill weed if desired. Serve with a green salad and green beans.

Darlene Fitzgerald
Grandbury, TX

Fast & Easy Spaghetti & Meatballs

1 lb. ground turkey or lean ground beef

2 c. Italian-style bread crumbs, or plain bread crumbs plus ½ tsp. Italian seasoning

1 T. Worcestershire sauce

½ c. grated Parmesan cheese

1 egg

½ tsp. salt

½ tsp. pepper

28-oz. jar spaghetti sauce (your favorite)

Combine ground meat, bread crumbs, Worcestershire sauce, Parmesan cheese, egg, salt and pepper in large bowl. Form mixture into meatballs and place on baking sheet sprayed with vegetable cooking spray. Bake at 400°F for 8 to 10 minutes. Turn meatballs over and bake for another 8 to 10 minutes.
Cook sauce in Dutch oven until heated through. Add cooked meatballs and simmer for 5 minutes before serving over cooked spaghetti noodles.

Irene O'Brien
Anchorage, AK

Quick Beef Stroganoff

1 lb. round steak, cut into ¾-inch cubes

Flour

2 T. fat

½ c. chopped onion

1 clove garlic, minced

6-oz. can mushrooms, drained with liquid reserved

1 c. sour cream

10¾-oz. can tomato soup

1 T. Worcestershire sauce

½ tsp. salt

Dash of pepper

Parmesan cheese

Dip meat in flour, brown in hot fat. Add onion, garlic and mushrooms. Combine sour cream, tomato soup, mushroom liquid and seasoning. Pour over meat.

Simmer for at least 1 hour or until tender. Serve over spaghetti, rice or noodles. Sprinkle with cheese.

Sharon Matheny
Van Wert, OH

Tom's Grilled Chicken Italiano

Large boneless grilled chicken breasts

Lean bacon

Kaiser rolls

Provolone cheese slices or cheese slices of choice

Oregano

Freshly ground pepper

Boiled ham, thinly sliced

¼ c. sliced mushrooms, sautéed

Cook chicken thoroughly on grill or in nonstick frying pan. Pat dry. Cook bacon (not too crisp), drain and pat dry. Cut roll in half and place cut side up on small baking sheet. Place 1 slice cheese on roll. Then chicken. Sprinkle with small amount of oregano and pepper. Place 3 to 4 slices of ham on chicken, then 3 to 4 slices bacon and mushrooms. Bake at 300°F until cheese melts. Remove and serve with fries.

Tom Cane
Norristown, PA

German-Style Pork Roast

1 tsp. salt

1 tsp. dry mustard

½ tsp. pepper

¼ T. flour

4-lb. pork loin roast

2 c. applesauce

½ c. brown sugar, packed

¼ tsp. cinnamon, ground

½ tsp. cloves, ground

1 lb. sauerkraut

Mix salt, mustard, pepper and flour. Rub over pork. Place pork fat side up in shallow roasting pan and bake at 350°F for 1 hour. Combine applesauce, brown sugar, cinnamon and cloves; spread ½ of mixture over top of pork and bake for an additional ½ hour. Spread remaining mixture over pork and return to oven for 15 minutes or until meat thermometer reads 185°F. Place sauerkraut around pork and place in oven for 45 minutes. Total cooking time: 2 hours 30 minutes.

Kurt Richter
Gretna, LA

Kim's Pizza

Pkg. rapid-rise yeast

1 c. lukewarm water

½ c. buttermilk

2 T. olive oil

2 T. sugar

½ tsp. salt

2½ to 3½ c. unbleached flour

Dissolve yeast in lukewarm water in small glass or plastic container. In 8-quart or larger mixing bowl, combine buttermilk, olive oil, sugar and salt. Add dissolved yeast to mixture in large bowl and gradually stir in flour, using smaller amount of flour first. Note: Air pressure, temperature and humidity all affect how much moisture flour will absorb. Adjust accordingly. Dough is ready when it forms a soft ball.

Lightly flour smooth surface and pour dough onto it. Flour hands and flatten dough by pushing away from yourself with the heels of your hands. Lift dough and fold in half; repeat flattening motion. Fold in half again and continue alternating the flattening and folding motions until dough is soft, smooth and springs back lightly when poked, about 8 minutes.

Top dough with your choice of items and bake on middle oven rack at a temperature between 400 and 450°F. Note: Your oven may not be perfectly calibrated; use an oven thermometer to test it. Remove pizza when it is a light golden brown, about 8 to 15 minutes.

Kimberly Stancil
Virginia Beach, VA

Chicken Mourenou

1 lb. chicken cutlets, cut into bite-size pieces

½ c. flour seasoned with salt and pepper, garlic, paprika

1 c. oil

1 c. white wine

28-oz. can whole tomatoes, chopped, with juice

6-oz. can black olives, sliced in half, or sliced mushrooms

Dip chicken into flour. Reserve 2 tablespoons flour for later. Heat oil. Fry chicken until golden brown. Transfer to ovenproof dish. Mix wine and reserved flour. Whisk until mixed well. In skillet, heat 2 tablespoons oil on medium high heat. Add wine mixture, tomatoes and olives; bring to a boil until thick. Pour over chicken. Cover with foil and bake for 350°F for 30 minutes. Serve over rice.

Martha Arango
Bronx, NY

Bourbon Sauce

1 c. ketchup

⅓ c. bourbon

¼ c. white vinegar

¼ c. molasses

2 cloves garlic, crushed

1 T. Worcestershire sauce

1 T. lemon juice

2 tsp. soy sauce

½ tsp. dry mustard

¼ tsp. black pepper

Combine ketchup, bourbon, vinegar, molasses, garlic, Worcestershire sauce, lemon juice, soy sauce, dry mustard and pepper, stirring well. This sauce does not need to be simmered. It is excellent for pork or beef.

Kelly Kutz
St. Petersburg, FL

Four Baked Bean Casserole

8 slices bacon

1 c. chopped onion

15-oz. can green beans (drained)

15-oz. can lima beans (drained)

15-oz. can kidney beans (use juice)

2 (15-oz.) cans pork and beans (use juice)

2 T. vinegar

¾ c. brown sugar

½ tsp. garlic salt

½ tsp. prepared mustard

⅛ tsp. pepper

Cook bacon crisp and cut it up. Sauté onion in bacon grease. Pour all beans into casserole; add bacon, onion and vinegar. Stir well, and bake covered for 45 minutes at 375°F. Or put them in slow cooker and cook on low for 6 to 8 hours.

Mary Gross
Bismarck, ND

Enchilada Hot Dish

2 lbs. hamburger

10¾-oz. can cream of mushroom soup

10¾-oz. can cream of chicken soup

can enchilada sauce

large can evaporated milk

flour tortillas

10-oz. pkg shredded taco cheese

Brown hamburger in large skillet. Add soups, enchilada sauce and milk. Heat hamburger mixture until thick. Line 9 x 13-inch pan with tortillas. Pour half of mixture onto tortillas. Add another layer of tortillas. Pour remaining mixture over tortillas. Bake at 350°F for 25 minutes. Top with cheese. Bake for 10 minutes more. Serve with your favorite taco sauce.

Amy Jo Gross
Bismarck, ND

Taco Pie

1 lb. hamburger

Pkg. taco seasoning

½ c. water

6-oz. can tomato sauce

8-oz. pkg. refrigerated crescent rolls

1 c. crushed tortilla chips, divided

1 c. sour cream

1 c. shredded cheddar cheese

Brown hamburger. Add taco seasoning, water and tomato sauce. Place crescent rolls in bottom of greased baking dish and flatten. Crumble half of chips over rolls. Pour meat mixture onto rolls and crushed chips. Smother with sour cream. Add cheese. Top with remaining chips. Bake for 20 to 25 minutes at 375°F. Serve with your favorite taco sauce.

Amy Jo Gross
Bismarck, ND

Peanut Butter Bars [109]

COOKIES
& bars

Sweet, luscious morsels abound here. These recipes—perfect for serving at parties or events, or for savoring as everyday treats—will indulge your taste buds (and your sweet tooth) at every bite!

Cowboy Cookies [101]

Cream Cheese Lemon Bars [100]

Faux Fireplace

We wanted a fireplace in the family room but there was no chimney. I designed a fireplace for the corner that uses electric logs and found a grate with an electric blower under it. It has really brought us a lot of cheer without the effort of hauling logs or cleaning ashes.

The front and top were made from pieces of the room paneling and trim. I found some brick wallpaper to cover the wood walls inside, which did not look right inside a fireplace. It measures 50 in. wide x 43 in. high. The top is 25 in. from the front to the corner. The opening is 27½ in. wide x 25½ in. high. The measurements are not critical but seem to be in proportion. Except for the electric logs and grate, the cost was minimal since it was all made from leftover paneling.

James Shields
Easton, MD

Honey Cookies

1⅓ c. oil

2 c. sugar

½ c. honey

2 eggs

2 tsp. vanilla

2 tsp. baking soda

1 tsp. salt

2 tsp. cinnamon

4½ c. flour

Cinnamon and sugar for rolling dough

Mix oil, sugar, honey, eggs and vanilla. Add soda, salt, cinnamon and flour. Roll into 1-inch balls, then in cinnamon sugar mixture. Place on baking sheet. Bake for 10 minutes at 350°F or until edges start to brown. If cooked longer, cookies will not be soft.

Paul & Diana Pritchett
Magna, UT

Turtle Brownies

14-oz. bag caramels

⅔ c. evaporated milk, divided

1 box German Chocolate cake mix

¾ c. margarine, softened

12-oz. bag chocolate chips

Combine caramels and ⅓ cup evaporated milk in double boiler. Stir until melted and well blended. Combine cake mix, ⅓ cup evaporated milk and margarine. Blend batter. Press half of cake mix into greased 9 x 13 pan. Bake for 6 minutes at 350°F. Remove from oven and sprinkle with chips. Top with melted caramels. Crumble remaining cake mix over caramel. Bake for 15 to 20 minutes at 350°F.

Amy Jo Gross
Bismarck, ND

Sensational Oatmeal Cookies

1 c. granulated sugar

½ c. butter, room temperature

¾ c. margarine, not imitation spread

1 c. dark molasses

2 eggs

1 tsp. vanilla

1½ c. flour

1 tsp. baking soda

1 tsp. salt, optional, or reduce to ¼ tsp.

1 tsp. cinnamon

¼ tsp. nutmeg

1 c. finely chopped walnuts

3 c. old-fashioned oats

1 c. raisins

Beat sugar, butter and margarine in large mixing bowl until fluffy. Add molasses and beat until fluffy again. Beat in eggs and vanilla. Combine flour, baking soda, salt and spices in smaller bowl. Add to molasses mixture and mix well. Mix nuts and oats together in small bowl and add to molasses mixture. Mix well. Add raisins and mix well.

Drop by rounded tablespoonfuls 2 inches apart onto ungreased baking sheet. Bake at 375°F for 11 to 13 minutes or until golden brown. Immediately remove from baking sheet with pancake turner and place on wire cooling rack.

Tip: Keep pancake turner clean and slip under cookie quickly in order to retain proper shape. Allow to cool on wire rack for 5 to 10 minutes before transferring to cookie jar or serving bowl.

James Kendrick
Novato, CA

Date Bars

2 T. margarine

1½ c. sugar

2 eggs

1 tsp. vanilla

1½ c. flour

2 tsp. baking powder

2 T. water

1 c. chopped dates

1 c. chopped nuts

Mix as you would a cake and put into 9 x 13-inch pan. Bake at 350°F for 20 minutes. Cut into bars and roll them in powdered sugar.

Margaret Reed
Portsmouth, OH

Super Peanut Butter Cookies

1 c. light corn syrup

1 c. sugar

1 c. peanut butter

6 to 7 c. Corn Flakes

Combine syrup and sugar. Bring to a boil, then add peanut butter. Put cereal in a large bowl. Pour peanut butter mixture over cereal and mix well. Drop by spoonfuls onto waxed paper.

Leona Matz
Galeton, PA

Deluxe Chocolate Marshmallow Bars

Deluxe Chocolate Marshmallow Bars

¾ c. butter or margarine

1½ c. sugar

3 eggs

1 tsp. vanilla

1⅓ c. flour

½ tsp. baking powder

½ tsp. salt

3 T. cocoa

½ c. nuts, optional

4 c. miniature marshmallows

1⅓ c. chocolate chips

3 T. butter or margarine

1 c. peanut butter

2 c. crispy rice cereal

In mixing bowl, combine butter and sugar. Add eggs and vanilla. Beat until fluffy. Add flour, baking powder, salt and cocoa. Stir in nuts if desired. Put in 9 x 13-inch pan. Bake at 350°F for 15 to 18 minutes.

Sprinkle marshmallows evenly over all. Cool completely in pan.

For topping, combine chocolate chips, butter and peanut butter in small saucepan. Cook over low heat, stirring constantly until melted and well blended. Remove from heat. Add cereal and mix well. Spread on top of marshmallows. Chill and serve.

Raymond Plank
Humboldt, IL

Easy Sugar Cookies

¾ c. sugar

⅓ c. margarine

⅓ c. oil

1 T. milk

1 to 2 tsp. vanilla, almond or your favorite flavor extract

1 egg

1½ c. flour

1½ tsp. baking powder

¼ tsp. salt

Colored sugar

Mix sugar, margarine, oil, milk, vanilla, egg, flour, baking powder and salt. Spread dough in greased and floured 8 x 10-inch pan. Sprinkle with colored sugar. Bake at 375°F for 12 to 15 minutes or until golden brown.

Paul & Diana Pritchett
Magna, UT

Brown Rim Cookies

1 c. shortening

1¾ c. sugar

2 eggs, well beaten

1½ tsp. vanilla

1 tsp. salt

1 tsp. baking powder

3½ c. flour

Cream shortening and sugar. Add eggs and vanilla. Combine salt, baking powder and flour. Sift into cream mixture and mix thoroughly. Roll dough into a ball and place on a greased baking sheet. Flatten with bottom of glass coated with grease or flour. Sprinkle lightly with sugar. Bake at 400°F for 8 to 10 minutes or until lightly browned rim appears.

Gary Mallon
Post Falls, ID

STATE-OF-THE-ART ENTERTAINMENT AREA

I have always been interested in electronics as a hobby, specifically audio and video equipment. I worked during high school as a projectionist at a drive-in and always thought of how I would like to have my own home theater. Needless to say this was a 15-year-think project. After moving into our new home, I stared at the bare concrete walls in the basement and started dreaming. I envisioned a high-quality projection system backed by state-of-the-art audio components to produce the most exhilarating entertainment experience possible.

The beam running perpendicular to the main beam is just to close the space and provide a spot to sort of hide the projector. In this photo you can see the door that allows access to the back of the equipment under the stairs. The doors to the cabi-

net are acrylic to prevent injury in case a partygoer is not paying attention. And of course the lighted exit sign is a must in any theater.

I could not find nor could I afford a cabinetmaker to build the custom speaker cabinets and screen surround, so I built this unit myself. It features a matte black Formica top and sides, removable speaker grills, pleated black velvet side curtains (which I sewed myself) and vents to allow for air circulation (the sump pump is hidden in the lower left cabinet). As

you can see, the unit provides an excellent focus for the theater and it doubles as a bench. The screen is electric and can be raised if necessary. In the up position I have access to another window and the fuse box. In case anyone asks, yes, there are speakers behind all of those grills. The little white thing in the upper left corner of the screen is the sensor for the screen remote. The grills are held by Velcro to allow easy removal. The crown molding at the top frames the screen and really finishes the space.

Screen surround and speaker cabinets.

Perpendicular beam.

Concession stand.

Utilizing space under staircase.

What is a theater without a concession stand? I put together these cabinets and countertop from leftover material, believe it or not. The doors and drawer fronts are purchased. I won the popper in an internet auction. The Pepsi logos on the fridge were next to impossible to get; I am still working on getting a regular pop machine. After the major work was done I switched to the finish items: black-and-white checker vinyl flooring, crown molding around dropped ceiling, all base molding, final electrical and carpeting.

The equipment installation was fun. We are talking about 5.1 Dolby Digital and DTS surround, digital component video and a raw 1,550 watts of power pushing eight speakers (my neighbors love me). All are high-grade interconnects and heavy duty speaker cables.

Here is a fun fact for you: When all of the equipment is fired up, it produces enough heat to warm the whole area. Fans behind the amps blow warm air out and a space at the top draws fresh air in. There is a DVD player, Hi-Fi VHS, satellite dish receiver, cassette deck, dual CD player (for the live DJ at my parties), amps and more.

I built a new staircase to help complete the room. The area under the stairs will be space for movie, CD, DVD and video tape storage shelves. The "L"-shaped bar has worked out great. Made with a leftover piece of Formica, it has edges finished with solid yellow pine just like a countertop. The supports are ½-in. black pipe with 1-in. footrests. The surround speakers fit nicely into the corners and the projector is safely out of the way. The movie reels hanging throughout are remnants from the drive-in I worked at in high school. The movie posters are originals from when I worked as a projectionist.

I used the Handyman Club books extensively, particularly when building the cabinetry. I used several of the joinery techniques I found in other volumes.

Peter Spyche
Lancaster, NY

Photography by Russell Halstead

The electronics system.

Cream Cheese Lemon Bars

Double-layer yellow cake mix

2 eggs, divided

⅓ c. vegetable oil

8-oz. pkg. cream cheese

⅓ c. sugar

1 T. lemon juice

Mix cake mix, 1 egg and vegetable oil until crumbly. Reserve 1 cup crumbs. Press remaining crumbs in lightly greased 9 x 13-inch pan. Bake at 350°F for 10 minutes.

Meanwhile, beat cream cheese, remaining egg, sugar and lemon juice until light and creamy. Spread on top of cake crust and sprinkle reserved crumbs on top. Return to oven and bake for 12 to 14 minutes. Cut into small squares when cooled.

David Kline
Sugarcreek, OH

Cream Cheese Lemon Bars & Cowboy Cookies

Cowboy Cookies

2 c. flour

1 tsp. baking soda

½ tsp. salt

½ tsp. baking powder

1 c. butter

1 c. sugar

1 c. brown sugar

1 tsp. vanilla

2 eggs

2 c. oatmeal

1 to 1½ c. chocolate chips

Sift flour, baking soda, salt and baking powder together. Set aside. Cream butter and sugars until well blended. Add vanilla, then eggs, one at a time, beating well after each addition. Stir in flour mixture just until blended. Add oatmeal and chocolate chips.

Drop by large tablespoons onto lightly greased baking sheet. Bake at 350°F for 12 minutes.

Kelly Carr
Novato, CA

Almond Bark Cookies

2 c. Special K cereal

2 c. crispy rice cereal

2 c. salted peanuts

2 c. miniature marshmallows

2-lb. pkg. almond bark

In large bowl, combine cereals, peanuts and marshmallows. Melt almond bark in top of double boiler. Pour melted almond bark over cereal mixture in bowl; mix. Drop by teaspoon onto waxed paper or buttered baking sheet. Allow to cool. Store in sealed container in cool place.

Mary Gross
Bismarck, ND

Peanut Butter Dream Bars

COOKIE LAYER

¾ c. firmly packed brown sugar

½ c. margarine, softened

¾ tsp. vanilla

1 egg

2 T. milk

2 c. baking mix

¾ c. cocoa

Combine all in large bowl. Mix with fork; mixture will be crumbly. Spray 9 x 13-inch pan with vegetable cooking spray. Press mixture into bottom of pan.

PEANUT BUTTER LAYER

8-oz. pkg. cream cheese or Neufchâtel cheese

1 c. peanut butter (any style)

½ c. brown sugar, firmly packed

1 egg

1 tsp. vanilla

2 T. milk

TOPPING

1 c. chocolate chips

In mixing bowl, cream together cheese and peanut butter until smooth. Beat in brown sugar, egg, vanilla and milk. Spread over cookie layer. Bake at 350°F for 25 minutes or until just set and bars begin to pull away from sides of pan.

Remove from oven. Sprinkle chocolate chips on top. After 5 minutes, chips will be soft. Spread with a spatula. Cool completely and cut into bars.

Tip: After bars have cooled to room temperature, pop them into fridge for 20 to 30 minutes to firm up chocolate layer.

Irene O'Brien
Anchorage, AK

Avalanche Cookies

2 c. crispy rice cereal

½ c. miniature marshmallows

¼ c. chocolate chips

6 oz. white chocolate chips

3 oz. peanut butter chips

1 oz. peanut butter

Mix cereal, marshmallows and chocolate chips. Melt white chocolate, peanut butter chips and peanut butter together. Add to cereal mixture and mix well. Drop in mounds on wax paper.

Margaret Reed
Portsmouth, OH

Seven-Layer Bars

½ c. butter

1 pkg. graham crackers, crushed

1 c. chocolate chips

1 c. butterscotch chips

1 c. white chocolate chips

1 c. chopped pecans

1 c. coconut

14-oz. can condensed milk

Melt butter in bread pan. Pour graham cracker crumbs into melted butter. In layers, add chocolate chips, then butterscotch chips, then white chocolate chips, then pecans, then coconut. Pour condensed milk over top. Bake at 350°F for 30 minutes. Remove from oven immediately. Allow to cool before cutting.

Brenda Watts
Nancy, KY

Creamy Lemon Macadamia Cookies

2 c. flour

½ tsp. baking soda

¼ tsp. salt

1 c. light brown sugar, packed

½ c. sugar

½ c. salted butter, softened

4-oz. pkg. cream cheese, softened

1 large egg

2 tsp. pure lemon extract or 1 tsp. vanilla plus 1 tsp. lemon zest

1½ c. whole macadamia nuts, unsalted

Preheat oven to 300°F. In a medium bowl, combine flour, soda and salt. Mix well and set aside. In a large bowl, blend sugars at medium mixer speed. Add butter and cream cheese and mix to form a smooth paste. Add egg and extract (plus zest if desired). Beat at medium speed until light and soft. Add flour mixture and blend at low speed until just combined. Stir in nuts.

Drop by rounded tablespoons onto ungreased sheets 2 inches apart. Bake for 23 to 25 minutes. Immediately transfer to a cool surface.

Lisa Krajnak
Lyndhurst, OH

LAKE-VIEW DECK-AND-ARBOR

Our new home is 75 feet or so above a lake and has a great spot on its shoreline where we can see two sections of the lake separated by an uninhabited peninsula. We planned this deck to be located outside the veranda accessed by the back door. It would be 25 ft. x 16 ft., and 8 ft. of its width would be covered with lattice to give protection from the sun and provide structure for climbing plants to make a natural cover.

Cement-block supports spaced every 4 ft. were used for the (6) treated 2-in. x 6-in. x 16-ft. supporting joints. I chose not to connect the deck to the house foundation, so the first supporting blocks were set about one foot from the slab. Before setting the blocks however, I first dug holes 18 in. deep for the (7) 4-in. x 4-in. posts which would support the lattice. I then cut the 4-in. x 4-in. posts so that the ones at the house were 9 ft. above the ground and tucked under the eaves; the outside posts were cut 8½ ft. above the ground, then cemented in to a depth of 18 in. I then

placed the cement supporting blocks and began the long process of setting each block so that each 16-ft. joist was level to the others and each had a 2-in. drop over the 16-ft. distance. I then installed 4-ft. joists between the 16-footers at 16-in. intervals to support the manufactured wood product, Trex, that I used for the decking.

The lattice arbor is made with 2-in. x 6-in. boards between the posts, installed lengthwise to the deck, and 2-in. x 4-in. rafters. I bolted (2) 2-in. x 6-in. pieces angled at 45° between the two mid posts at the house and the joist across the top of the post, and (2) between the two outermost back posts and the outermost rafters at each end. This increased the stability of the entire overhead structure. I installed 4-ft. x 8-ft. lattice panels

across the rafters.

No railings were installed as the deck is only 6 in. off the ground and they would block some of the view. Mirrored Plexiglas was placed around each of the outside posts to lessen their visibility, which worked out quite well. I used a long string of white outdoor Christmas lights strung around the inside top in lieu of a standard porch light, which gives a nice subtle lighting effect. We are looking forward to some great leisure hours and to enjoying beautiful sunsets in the future!

**Carmond Fitzgerald
Granbury, TX**

Applesauce Cookies

2 c. flour

1 tsp. salt

¾ tsp. baking soda

½ tsp. cinnamon

¼ tsp. cloves

1½ c. brown sugar, firmly packed

1 c. shortening

2 eggs

1 c. applesauce

1½ c. rolled oats

1 c. raisins

1 c. chopped nuts, optional

Sift flour, salt, soda, cinnamon and cloves together into a bowl. Cream sugar and shortening. Add eggs and applesauce; beat until smooth. Add flour mixture; stir in oats, raisins and nuts. Drop by teaspoons onto greased baking sheet. Bake for 15 minutes at 350°F.

**Margaret Reed
Portsmouth, OH**

Caramel Cream Sandwich Cookies

¾ c. brown sugar, firmly packed

1 c. butter or margarine, room temperature

1 egg yolk, unbeaten

2¾ c. flour

2 T. butter or margarine, room temperature

1¼ c. sifted powdered sugar

½ T. vanilla

4 to 5 T. cream

Gradually add brown sugar to 1 cup butter and cream together well. Blend in egg yolk. Add flour and stir until mixture forms dough. Chill if necessary for easy handling. Shape into marble-sized balls. Place on ungreased baking sheet and flatten to ⅛-inch thickness with palm of hand. Make a design on top by pressing with fork in one direction. Bake at 325°F for 8 to 10 minutes until cookies begin to brown very lightly. Remove from baking sheet while warm.

Meanwhile, prepare frosting. Brown 2 tablespoons butter in saucepan. Remove from heat and blend in powdered sugar. Gradually add vanilla and cream; stir until of spreading consistency.

When cookies have cooled, frost flat sides and put together to make a cookie sandwich. Cookies are also good without frosting.

**Russell DeLancey
Leavittsburg, OH**

Applesauce Cookies

Caramel Cream Sandwich Cookies

Peanut Clusters

Peanut Munch Bars

Peanut Munch Bars

Double-layer yellow cake mix

1 c. butter or margarine, divided

1 egg

3 c. miniature marshmallows

12-oz. pkg. peanut butter chips

½ c. corn syrup

12-oz. pkg. peanuts

1½ c. crispy rice cereal

Mix cake mix, ½ cup butter and egg. Press into 9 x 13-inch pan. Bake at 350°F for 10 to 12 minutes. Spread marshmallows on top of crust and bake for another 3 minutes. Cool.

Melt chips, syrup and ½ cup butter. Add peanuts and cereal. Spread over crust. When cool, cut into bars.

Joyce Melcher
Isanti, MN

Peanut Clusters

12-oz. pkg. chocolate chips

1 lb. white almond bark

1 lb. salted, oven-roasted peanuts

Melt chips and bark in microwave for 3 to 5 minutes, stirring often, until softened. Add peanuts. Spoon onto waxed paper and let cool.

Tim & Tammy Kriesel
Russellville, AR

Salted Nut Chew Bars

1½ c. flour

½ tsp. baking powder

1/4 tsp. baking soda

½ tsp. salt

⅔ c. brown sugar

¾ c. butter, softened, divided

2 egg yolks

3 tsp. vanilla, divided

3 c. miniature marshmallows

⅔ c. corn syrup

2 c. peanut butter chips

2 c. crispy rice cereal

1½ c. salted peanuts

Combine flour, baking powder, baking soda and salt. In separate large bowl, combine brown sugar, ½ cup butter, egg yolks and 1 teaspoon vanilla. Add flour mixture to brown sugar mixture; stir until well blended. Press batter into greased 9 x 13-inch pan. Bake at 350°F for 10 to 12 minutes. Sprinkle marshmallows over top and return bars to oven for 1 to 2 minutes (until marshmallows puff). Allow to cool while preparing topping.

For topping, heat corn syrup, ¼ cup butter, vanilla and chips until smooth. Remove from heat and stir in cereal and salted peanuts. Immediately spread topping over marshmallow layer. Allow to cool before serving.

Mary Gross
Bismarck, ND

Lime Surprise

12-oz. can evaporated milk

Pkg. lime gelatin

¼ c. lime juice

2 tsp. lemon juice

1 c. sugar

2 c. Oreo cookie crumbs

⅓ c. butter, melted

Chill evaporated milk in freezer until ice cold. Dissolve gelatin mix in 1¾ cups hot water. Chill gelatin until partially cooled and set. Whip gelatin until fluffy. Stir in lime and lemon juices and sugar. In separate bowl, whip milk and fold into gelatin mixture.

Combine Oreo crumbs and butter. Press crumb mixture into 9 x 13-inch pan. Pour gelatin mixture over crumbs. Chill until firm. Garnish top with shaved chocolate and chopped pecans.

Mary Gross
Bismarck, ND

Chuck's Favorite Chocolate Cookies

3 c. wheat flakes cereal

Pkg. German sweet chocolate

1-oz. square baker's chocolate

1 tsp. butter

Put cereal in large bowl and use your hands to crunch cereal flakes into small bits. Melt chocolate and butter either in microwave or in top of a double boiler on stove. Add melted chocolate mixture to cereal; stir until cereal is well coated. Drop by teaspoons onto waxed paper. Allow to cool. Store in airtight container.

Rosemary Koshiol
Paynesville, MN

Sarah's Secret Recipe for Soft Chocolate Chip Cookies

1 lb. (4 sticks) butter, softened

2 eggs

2 T. molasses

2 tsp. vanilla

⅓ c. water

1½ c. sugar

1½ c. brown sugar

1 tsp. baking powder

1½ tsp. baking soda

1 tsp. salt

5 c. flour

1½ (12-oz.) pkgs. semi sweet chocolate chips

Preheat oven to 375°F. In large bowl, cream together butter, eggs, molasses, vanilla and water. In separate bowl, combine sugars, baking powder, baking soda, salt and flour. Add sugar mixture to creamed butter mixture; mix well. Add chocolate chips; stir.

Shape dough into 1-inch balls. Place 1 inch apart on ungreased baking sheet. Bake for 8 minutes or until light brown around edges.

Sarah Davis
Abbs Valley, VA

Peanut Butter Bars

$\mathcal{P}$eanut Butter Bars

1 c. chunky peanut butter

½ c. melted butter

2 large eggs

Double-layer yellow cake mix

6 oz. semisweet chocolate chips

14-oz. can sweetened condensed milk

Combine peanut butter, butter, eggs and cake mix in large bowl. Beat for 2 minutes at medium speed with mixer. Lightly grease 9-inch pan. Press half of mixture into bottom of pan. Bake at 350°F for 10 minutes. Sprinkle with chocolate chips, drizzle milk over mixture in pan. Sprinkle remainder of mixture on top. Bake at 350°F for 30 minutes. Cool on wire rack.

Tim & Tammy Kriesel
Russellville, AR

Chocolate Biscuits [page 122]

Pecan Tassies [page 135]

PIES, CAKES
& other desserts

A recipe for every kind of pie, cake or confection you can imagine seems to be included in this final chapter. These sweet ideas make any occasion more festive ... even an everyday meal.

Apple Coffee Cake [page 139]

Snow Gauge

As a true Minnesotan, I had always enjoyed measuring the new snowfall and tracking the amount of snow accumulated on the ground. I had always thought about a snow gauge, but never pursued having one.

When I retired, I decided that was a good project and started looking for patterns. When I did not find one, I sat down and started sketching. Once I had the idea, I showed it to my husband and the two of us got busy creating.

Rachel Pfaffendorf
Stacy, MN

Best Rhubarb Shortcake

6 c. cut-up rhubarb

¾ c. sugar

3 T. margarine

1 c. flour

1 tsp. baking powder

¼ tsp. salt

½ c. milk

2¾-oz. pkg. strawberry gelatin mix

1 c. sugar

2 T. cornstarch

¼ tsp. salt

1 c. boiling water

Spread rhubarb in bottom of 8 x 8-inch pan. Cream ¾ cup sugar with margarine. Add flour, baking powder and salt. Mix well. Add milk. Mix well and spread over rhubarb. Sprinkle with gelatin mix powder. Combine 1 cup sugar, cornstarch and salt. Sprinkle over top. Pour water over all. Bake at 350°F for 1 hour.

Leona Matz
Galeton, PA

Quick Pie Crust

1½ c. flour

1 tsp. salt

1½ tsp. sugar

½ c. oil

2 T. milk

Mix together and pat out in pie pan. Bake for 8 to 10 minutes at 375°F. Great for cream pies.

Margaret Reed
Portsmouth, OH

Ice Cream Dessert

2½ c. crushed Rice Chex cereal

½ c. melted butter

1 c. flaked coconut

1 c. brown sugar

1 c. chopped cashews

½ gal. vanilla ice cream

Mix cereal, butter, coconut, brown sugar and cashews together. Put half of cereal mixture into 9 x 13-inch pan. Spread ½ gallon ice cream over mixture and top with remaining mixture. Freeze until hard.

Mrs. LeRoy Hagert
Springfield, MN

Chocolate-Dipped Cinnamon Crisps

Pkg. 6-in. flour tortillas

½ c. semisweet chocolate chips

1 T. shortening

½ c. sugar

1 tsp. cinnamon

Cut each tortilla into wedges and lay on ungreased baking sheets. Bake at 400°F for 4 to 7 minutes or until golden brown. In small saucepan over low heat, melt chocolate chips and shortening, stirring constantly.

Remove from heat and place pan in warm water to keep chocolate soft, or use double boiler. Line baking sheets with waxed paper. In plastic bag, combine sugar and cinnamon. Gently shake a few wedges at a time in mixture. Dip wide end of wedge in melted chocolate. Place on waxed paper. Refrigerate until chocolate is set.

Teri Hogan
Mico, TX

Nutty Apple Dip

8-oz. pkg. cream cheese, room temperature

¾ c. brown sugar

1 tsp. vanilla

1 c. chopped salted peanuts

Apples

Orange juice

Blend cream cheese, brown sugar, vanilla and peanuts together. Wash and slice apples; dip in orange juice. Drizzle orange juice over apples on serving plate and sprinkle some chopped peanuts on top of dip before serving. Refrigerate any leftovers.

Mrs. David Kline
Sugarcreek, OH

Hot Fudge Sauce

1 c. cocoa

1 T. flour, heaping

2 c. sugar

1⅔ c. milk

6 T. butter

½ tsp. salt

¼ c. butter

Mix cocoa, flour and sugar thoroughly. Add milk and 6 tablespoons butter. Bring to a boil for 1 minute, stirring constantly. Remove from heat and beat well. Stir in salt and ¼ cup butter. Store in refrigerator. Heat before serving. Makes about 1 pint.

Char Salzbrun
Coon Rapids, MN

Lemon Silk Pie & Creamy Fruit Dip

Lemon Silk Pie

14-oz. can sweetened condensed milk

6-oz. can frozen lemonade, defrosted

3 tsp. lemon juice

5 drops yellow or red food coloring

16-oz. tub whipped topping

9-inch pie crust

Mix milk, lemonade, juice and food coloring. Add whipped topping and mix well. Fill pie shell and chill. Garnish with toasted coconut, if desired.

Margaret Reed
Portsmouth, OH

Carrot & Pineapple Bread

3 eggs, beaten

2 c. sugar

1 c. cooking oil

1 c. carrots, grated

20-oz. can crushed pineapple, not drained

1 c. chopped nuts

1½ tsp. cinnamon

1 tsp. salt

1 tsp. soda

3 c. flour

2 tsp. vanilla

Mix eggs, sugar, oil, carrots and pineapple. Add nuts, cinnamon, salt, soda, flour and vanilla. Mix well and put into 2 loaf pans. Bake at 325°F for 1 hour.

Leona Matz
Galeton, PA

Creamy Fruit Dip

8-oz. pkg. cream cheese, room temperature

7 oz. marshmallow cream

Mix cream cheese and marshmallow cream together and chill.

Serve with a variety of fruits. Dip apples and banana slices in orange or pineapple juice to keep them from turning brown.

David Kline
Sugarcreek, OH

Easy Fudge

20 oz. milk chocolate chips

14-oz. can sweetened condensed milk

½ c. walnuts, optional

Soften chocolate chips in a large microwaveable bowl. Stir in milk and walnuts. Pour into pan. Let set.

Raymond Myers
DeWitt, IA

"Repurposed" Hoosier Cabinet

About ten years ago I came across an original Hoosier cabinet in the basement of a friend's house. Although it had several coats of paint, all the glue joints were loose and some the wood was beyond repair, it still brought back memories of my mother's kitchen in the 1930s. It had copper hinges with copper screws, a flour bin, a metal bread drawer and all of the original metal clips and holders.

It looked like new when it was refinished, but I didn't know what to do with it since there was no room for it in our kitchen. I finally decided to convert it into a TV center. I added a TV table with a shelf for a VCR and two overhead cabinet doors that matched the originals. Since our living room has a twenty-foot-high A-frame ceiling, the cabinet looked too short, so I added a cap across the top.

T. J. Thomas
Cincinnati, OH

Editor's Note: Refurbishing or restoring antique furniture is a fun activity that can yield some very satisfying results. In most cases, the best reason to undertake a project like T. J.'s is to make something that was basically useless into something that has a place in your home. But before you decide to launch into a restoration project, it's always a good idea to talk to an antiques expert about your plans. Bring a photo to any dealer and see what he or she thinks. You may find that the piece you have plans for is valuable or rare. If so, even the simplest refurbishing, like stripping and refinishing the wood, can greatly decrease the value.

Never-Fail Pie Crust

Makes 2 double crusts

    3 c. flour
    1 c. lard or shortening
    1 tsp. salt
    ¼ c. water
    1 egg, beaten
    1 tsp. vinegar

Mix flour, lard, salt and water. Add egg and vinegar. Form into 4 flattened disks and refrigerate for 30 minutes before rolling out.

Mrs. LeRoy Hagert
Springfield, MN

Coffee Time Grable (Doughnuts)

    2 eggs
    1 c. sugar
    1 c. milk
    1 T. baking powder
    1½ tsp. salt
    1 T. allspice
    4 c. flour

Mix eggs, sugar, milk, baking powder, salt, allspice and flour. Roll out to ½ inch thick. Cut in strips or any shape desired. Deep-fry.

Henry Huber
McPherson, KS

Sherry Cake

    Double-layer yellow cake mix
    3.4-oz. pkg. vanilla instant pudding
    1 tsp. nutmeg
    4 eggs
    ¾ c. oil
    ¾ c. sherry
    Powdered sugar

Combine cake mix, pudding mix and nutmeg. Add eggs, oil and sherry. Beat on low speed of mixer until blended. Then beat at high speed for 10 minutes.

Pour mixture into ungreased and unfloured angel food cake pan. Bake at 375°F for 50 to 60 minutes.

Cake is done when toothpick inserted in center comes out clean. Invert pan and cool completely. Dust with powdered sugar.

Kelly J. Carr
Novato, CA

Quick 'N Easy Snacks

    2 c. powdered nonfat dry milk
    ½ c. peanut butter, smooth or crunchy
    ½ c. honey or syrup or jelly
    Chopped nuts, raisins, coconut, optional

Mix powdered milk, peanut butter and honey until consistency of soft dough. Add nuts, raisins or coconut. Shape into logs and slice or spoon into balls. Roll in chopped nuts or coconut if desired. High calorie but nutritious.

LaDonna Kolman Reyes
Hamilton, MO

Black Forest Pie

Black Forest Pie

8-oz. tub whipped topping, divided

9-in. baked pie crust

1 c. milk

3.4-oz. pkg. instant chocolate pudding

1 c. cherry pie filling

Spread 1 cup whipped topping on bottom of pie crust. Combine milk and pudding. Mix well, then fold in 1½ cups whipped topping. Spread pudding mixure over whipped topping in crust. Put remaining whipped topping on pudding layer, then spoon cherries on top. Garnish with chocolate curls. Chill and serve.

David Kline
Sugarcreek, OH

Banana Split Cheesecake

Box no-bake cheesecake mix

3 to 4 bananas

8-oz. can crushed pineapple, drained

6-oz. pkg. chopped nuts

8-oz. tub whipped topping

Maraschino cherries

In 9 x 9-inch pan, prepare cheesecake crust according to directions; press firmly with fingers. Slice bananas and place enough slices to cover crust; set aside. Make cheesecake filling according to package directions and pour over bananas. Sprinkle crushed pineapple and nuts over cheese filling. Spread whipped topping over top. Garnish with cherries on top. Keep refrigerated.

Frank Kuykendall
Rochester, WA

Lemonade Pie

6 oz. frozen lemonade concentrate, defrosted

14-oz. can sweetened condensed milk

8-oz. tub whipped topping

Graham cracker crust

Mix lemonade and milk. Fold whipped topping into lemonade mixture. Pour filling into crust and chill.

Mrs. LeRoy Hagert
Springfield, MN

Dum-Dum Salad

15¼-oz. can crushed pineapple

21-oz. can cherry pie filling

14-oz. can sweetened condensed milk

12½-oz. can of nuts

8-oz. tub whipped topping

Combine pineapple, pie filling, milk and nuts and mix well. Refrigerate for 2 hours. Add whipped topping. Mix well. Refrigerate until served. Garnish with chopped nuts if desired.

Terry & Donna Nunley
Gruetli, TN

Self-Filled Cupcakes

Double-layer Devil's Food cake mix

8-oz. pkg. cream cheese, softened

⅓ c. sugar

1 egg

6 oz. semisweet chocolate chips

Prepare cake batter according to package directions. Fill paper baking cups in muffin tins ⅔ full. Cream together cheese and sugar. Beat in egg. Stir in chocolate chips. Drop a rounded teaspoonful of cheese mixture into each cupcake. Bake per package directions for cupcakes.

Teri Hogan
Mico, TX

Pretzel Gelatin

2 c. crushed pretzels

¾ c. melted margarine

3 T. sugar

8-oz. pkg. cream cheese

1 c. sugar

16-oz. tub whipped topping, divided

6-oz. pkg. strawberry gelatin

2 c. boiling water

2 (10-oz.) pkgs. frozen sugared strawberries

For crust, combine pretzels, margarine and sugar; pack into 9 x 13-inch baking pan. Bake at 400°F for 8 minutes. Allow to cool.

In the meantime, beat cream cheese, sugar and half of whipped topping until smooth. Spread over cooled crust. Chill until firm.

Dissolve gelatin mix in boiling water. Add strawberries and pour over cream cheese layer. Chill until firm. Top with remaining whipped topping.

Lorraine Bell
Boron, CA

Mild (Light on the Spices) Pumpkin Pie

½ c. sugar

¼ c. brown sugar

1 T. cornstarch

½ tsp. salt

¼ tsp. ginger

2 eggs, beaten

12-oz. can evaporated milk

1½ c. canned pumpkin

1 tsp. vanilla

9-in. unbaked pie shell

Combine sugars, cornstarch, salt and ginger. In separate bowl, mix eggs, milk, pumpkin and vanilla. Add sugar mixture and mix well. Pour into unbaked pie shell. Bake at 425°F for 15 minutes, then 350°F for 45 minutes.

Leona Matz
Galeton, PA

No-Fat Ice Cream

½ gal. skim milk

14-oz. can fat-free condensed milk

3 tsp. vanilla

⅔ c. sugar (or sweeten to taste)

Pinch of salt

Peaches or strawberries for flavor if desired

Pour milk, condensed milk and vanilla into bowl. Measure sugar and add salt; mix. Combine sugar with milk mixture; pour into ice cream freezer container. Freeze for approximately 45 minutes in electric ice cream freezer.

Harry Miller
Albemarle, NC

WALNUT-LOOK ENTERTAINMENT CENTER

This is the entertainment center I made to fit my TV, VCR and electronic components. It is made of ¾-in. birch plywood, and all shelves on the right are adjustable except the middle one. The edges have iron-on walnut edge tape.

Billy Jones
Maryville, TN

Editor's Note: Birch plywood is one of the best sheet goods for building furniture. It has very smooth, low-figure grain that is perfect for painting. Or, you can follow Billy's lead and stain it—birch can be stained to imitate more expensive wood types. By using a walnut stain and walnut edge tape, Billy has created the look of solid walnut for a fraction of the price.

Chocolate Biscuits

2 c. flour

½ tsp. salt

3 tsp. double-acting baking powder

6 T. chilled butter

1 c. chocolate chips

¾ c. milk

Preheat oven to 450°F. Sift flour, salt and baking powder together. Cut in butter to make flaky mixture. In separate microwave dish, melt chocolate chips for approximately 1 to 2 minutes, being careful not to overheat. Stir well. Make a well in the flaky mixture. Pour in melted chips and milk. Stir until dough is fairly free from sides of bowl. Turn dough onto lightly floured board. Knead gently and quickly, making about eight to ten folds. Roll with lightly floured rolling pin until dough has desired thickness. Cut with biscuit cutter dipped in very little flour. Brush tops with milk or butter. Place on ungreased baking sheet and bake for 12 to 15 minutes at 450°F.

Sharleen Taira
Gardena, CA

Chocolate Biscuits

Molded Ambrosia

9 oz. crushed pineapple

2¾-oz. pkg. sugar-free orange gelatin

⅓ c. sugar

1 c. hot water

1 c. graham cracker crumbs

¼ c. light margarine, melted

1 c. fat-free dairy sour cream

¼ tsp. vanilla

11-oz. can mandarin oranges

½ c. flaked coconut

Maraschino cherries, optional

Drain pineapple, reserving syrup; set pineapple aside. Dissolve gelatin and sugar in hot water. Stir in reserved pineapple syrup. Chill until partially set.

Combine crumbs and margarine; reserve ⅓ cup for topping. Press remaining crumb mixture into 8 x 8-inch baking dish. Add sour cream and vanilla to partially set gelatin. Whip until fluffy.

Fold in pineapple, oranges and coconut. Pour mixture over crumbs in dish. Sprinkle top with reserved crumbs and chill until firm. Cut into squares and trim with maraschino cherries if desired.

Teri Hogan
Mico, TX

Peanut Clusters

24-oz. pkg. vanilla-flavored almond bark, broken into pieces

12-oz. pkg. chocolate chips

2 (16-oz.) pkgs. salted peanuts (or dry-roasted peanuts, cocktail peanuts or mixed nuts)

Mix almond bark and chips in mixing bowl. Microwave for 1 to 2 minutes. Stir. Do 1 minute intervals so chocolate doesn't burn. Melt until smooth; stirring helps. Add peanuts and mix well. Spoon onto baking sheet with teaspoon. Freeze for 5 to 10 minutes or longer if needed. Cluster will slide right off when frozen. If they stick a little, it is okay to scrape them off. Put clusters in a container and store in a cool place. Enjoy!

Robin Young
Bennington, NE

Grandma's Apple Crisp

5 Granny Smith apples

1 tsp. ground cinnamon

2 T. flour

½ c. sugar

1 c. flour

½ c. brown sugar

2 T. sugar

½ c. butter, softened

Peel, core and thinly slice apples. Mix cinnamon, 2 tablespoons flour and ½ cup sugar in a small bowl. Mix well with apple slices until slices are well coated. Pour apple mixture into 8 x 8-inch pan. Mix 1 cup flour, brown sugar, 2 tablespoons sugar and butter; pour over apple mixture. Spread topping evenly over apples. Bake at 450°F for 15 minutes. It may smell like it is burning the first few minutes; this is normal. Continue baking for the full 15 minutes. Reduce heat to 350°F and bake for an additional 22 minutes. Allow to cool before serving.

Mike Flinn
Shawnee Mission, KS

The project is a remodeling project where we added a 12-ft. x 24-ft. room to our house and turned our old living room into a his/hers computer work station/library.

All of the carpentry and roofing, electrical, siding and interior finishing were done by my son and me. The exceptions are the carpet laying (done professionally) and the rag-roll painting of the walls (done by a painter friend who leases our property for deer hunting). The project took about seven months of spare-time work (my son and I are both professional handymen).

Some of the highlights of the adventure were removing an old brick chimney, installing an energy-efficient furnace, rerouting the gas water heater piping, tying the new roof into the old, and working around projects for customers, and waiting for appropriate weather opportunities.

**Dale Netherton
Farmington, IA**

Peanut Butter-Chocolate Cheesecake

CRUST

1½ c. graham cracker crumbs

½ c. light brown sugar

½ c. melted butter

Mix crumbs and sugar. Add butter. Mix well. If too dry, add more butter. Press into bottom and up sides of 9- or 10-inch springform pan. Refrigerate until filling is ready.

FILLING

2 (8-oz.) pkgs. cream cheese, room temperature

2 c. creamy peanut butter

2 c. sugar

2 tsp. vanilla

2 or 3 T. melted butter

1½ c. heavy cream, whipped

In large bowl, add cheese, peanut butter, sugar, vanilla and butter. Mix for 5 minutes or until smooth and creamy. In small bowl, whip cream until soft peaks form. Fold into cream cheese mixture until you can no longer see any white. Pour into prepared pan and smooth top evenly with a butter knife or spatula. Chill for at least 8 hours or overnight.

TOPPING

4 oz. semisweet chocolate, melted

3 T. plus 2 tsp. hot coffee

¼ c. heavy cream

Melt chocolate with coffee in top of double boiler. When chocolate is melted, slowly add cream, stirring until smooth and creamy. Pour over top of chilled cake. Rotate pan in circular motion to cover top of cake evenly. Chill until firm, approximately 30 minutes. Can be frozen and served straight from the freezer.

Deborah Schilling
Basking Ridge, NJ

Pecan Pie

1 c. sugar

2 T. self-rising flour

Dash of salt

2 T. butter

3 eggs

¾ c. light corn syrup

¾ c. pecans, chopped

1 tsp. vanilla

9-in. unbaked pie crust

Mix sugar, flour and salt together well. Melt butter. Add eggs to butter and beat vigorously. Combine sugar mixture and butter mixture. Add corn syrup. Add pecans and vanilla. Pour into pie shell. Bake for 45 minutes at 325°F. Variation: You can top pie with pecans instead of including pecans in batter.

Brenda Watts
Nancy, KY

Eggnog Pie

5.9-oz. pkg. instant vanilla pudding

2½ c. eggnog

9-in. graham cracker crust

Nutmeg

Prepare pudding as directed, using eggnog instead of milk. Pour pudding mixture into pie crust. Sprinkle with nutmeg and chill for 1 hour before serving.

Paul & Diana Pritchett
Magna, UT

Dirt Dessert

1½ large bags Oreo cookies

4 c. milk

2 (3.4-oz.) pkgs. vanilla instant pudding

12-oz. tub whipped topping

¾ stick butter or margarine, softened

8-oz. pkg. cream cheese, softened

⅓ c. powdered sugar

Crush Oreos. In a separate bowl, mix milk and pudding until thick. Allow to set. Fold in whipped topping. Cream butter and cream cheese. Add powdered sugar and continue to cream. Blend this mixture into pudding mixture.

Line a flowerpot with plastic wrap. Begin filling with a layer of crushed cookies, then pudding mixture. Continue to layer, ending with cookies on top. I make wooden tulips with long stems (wrapped with plastic wrap) to "plant" in the "dirt" and then garnish with some gummy worms. I make enough flowers so each person at the table can take one home as a memento of the occasion.

Deborah Schilling
Basking Ridge, NJ

Jim's Tropical Fruit Cake

2½ c. cake flour

2 T. baking powder

½ tsp. baking soda

½ tsp. salt

½ c. butter, softened

½ c. sugar

4 large eggs

½ c. mashed ripe banana

½ c. crushed pineapple with juice

½ c. kiwi, peeled and sliced

½ c. golden raisins

½ c. grated, flaked coconut

½ c. chopped walnuts

¼ tsp. ground cloves

½ tsp. nutmeg

1 tsp. cinnamon

1 c. milk

LEMON GLAZE

½ c. butter

1½ c. powdered sugar

Zest of 1 lemon

Juice of 1 lemon

Mix flour, baking powder, baking soda and salt. Cream flour mixture together with butter, sugar and eggs. Blend banana, pineapple, kiwi, raisins, coconut and walnuts in blender or processor. Mix fruit and flour mixtures together. Add spices and milk. Blend together thoroughly. Pour into greased and floured bundt pan.

Bake at 350°F for 60 to 70 minutes. When a wooden toothpick inserted in cake's center comes out clean, cake is done. Let cool on rack for 15 minutes before removing from pan. Let cool completely on wire rack.

Meanwhile, mix butter, powdered sugar, lemon zest and lemon juice for Lemon Glaze. When cake has cooled, top with Lemon Glaze, letting it run down sides.

James Bray Sr.
Fresno, CA

Jim's Tropical Fruit Cake

Summer Delight

2 (12-count) boxes ice cream sandwiches

12-oz. tub whipped topping

12 oz. chocolate chips (or shredded chocolate bark)

Chocolate syrup

Place sandwiches in bottom of square or rectangular glass pan. Cover with layer of whipped topping. Place another layer of sandwiches on top and cover with remaining whipped topping. Sprinkle top with chocolate chips and drizzle chocolate syrup over all as desired. Suggestions for other additions: cherries, chopped pecans, M&Ms, crushed Oreos. Whatever you may like.

Jeffrey D. Barrilleaux
Thibodaux, LA

Mandarin Orange Cake

Double-layer yellow cake mix

½ c. oil

4 eggs

16-oz. can mandarin oranges, undrained

FROSTING

16-oz. tub whipped topping

8-oz. can crushed pineapple

3.4-oz pkg. instant vanilla pudding

Combine cake mix, oil, eggs and oranges. Pour mixture into greased 9 x 13-inch pan. Bake at 350°F for 35 to 40 minutes. Allow to cool.

In the meantime, prepare frosting: mix whipped topping, pineapple and pudding mix.

Wayne Jensen
American Falls, ID

Potato-Choc-Raisin Cake

2 c. sugar

1 c. butter or margarine

1 c. milk

3 T. cocoa

2 c. flour

1 c. raisins

1 c. pecans

1 c. mashed potatoes

1 tsp. cinnamon

1 tsp. allspice

2 tsp. baking powder

FROSTING

⅓ c. butter

4 or 5 T. water

¼ c. powdered milk

½ c. cocoa

2½ c. powdered sugar

1 tsp. vanilla

Prepare cake batter: Cream sugar, butter, milk and cocoa. Add flour, raisins, pecans, potatoes, spices and baking powder. Bake at 350°F for 30 minutes. Allow cake to cool before frosting.

To prepare frosting, cream butter with water. Add powdered milk, cocoa and sugar. Mix well. Add vanilla; mix well.

Dorothy Ellebracht
Blanco, TX

Impossible Pumpkin Pie

2 eggs

½ c. baking mix

12- to 13-oz. can evaporated milk, add water to make 2 c.

15-oz. can pumpkin

¾ c. sugar

2 T. butter

1 tsp. cinnamon

½ tsp. salt

½ tsp. ginger

¼ tsp. cloves

¼ tsp. nutmeg

Combine eggs, baking mix, milk, pumpkin, sugar, butter, cinnamon, salt, ginger, cloves and nutmeg in blender and mix for 2 minutes. Pour into greased and floured 9- to 10-inch glass pie pan. Bake at 350°F for 40 to 50 minutes.

Henry Kruschek Jr.
Waunakee, WI

Crazy Cake

1 c. sugar

1½ c. flour

½ tsp. salt

¼ c. cocoa

1 tsp. baking powder

1 c. cold water

⅓ c. oil

1 T. vinegar

1 tsp. vanilla

Sift dry ingredients into 9-inch ungreased baking pan. Make 3 wells in dry ingredients. Place each of the following in its own well: water, oil and vinegar. Add vanilla to water well. Stir batter until evenly mixed. Bake at 350°F for 30 to 45 minutes.

Dorothy Ellebracht
Blanco, TX

Pralines

Butter for greasing pan

¾ c. light brown sugar

¾ c. sugar

¾ c. half-and-half

3 T. butter or margarine

1¼ c. coarsely chopped pecans

½ c. vanilla

Grease bottom of heavy 3-quart saucepan with butter. Cook sugars, half-and-half and 3 tablespoons butter in saucepan over low heat, stirring occasionally for 6 to 8 minutes or until candy thermometer registers 238°F (soft-ball stage). Remove from heat. Stir in pecans and vanilla. Let stand for 3 minutes. Beat with a wooden spoon for 3 minutes or until mixture begins to thicken. Working rapidly, drop by tablespoons onto waxed paper. Let stand until firm.

Donna Miller
Collierville, TN

Chocolate Roll-Ups

½ c. (3 oz.) semisweet chocolate chips

1 T. vegetable shortening

1 tsp. almond extract

8-oz. pkg. refrigerated crescent rolls

2 T. sliced almonds

Powdered sugar

Combine chips and shortening in small saucepan. Cook over low heat, stirring constantly until mixture is melted and smooth. Remove from heat and stir in almond extract. Unroll crescent roll dough and separate into 8 triangles. Spread chocolate evenly over each triangle and sprinkle with sliced almonds. Cut each triangle in half and roll up, starting at wide end. Place rolls on baking sheet and bake for 12 to 15 minutes at 350°F or until golden brown. Sprinkle with powdered sugar and serve.

Donna Miller
Collierville, TN

Lewis's Cheesecake

$\mathscr{L}$ewis's Cheesecake

1½ c. graham cracker crumbs

¼ c. brown sugar, packed

⅓ c. margarine, melted

12 oz. cream cheese, softened

½ c. sugar

¼ tsp. vanilla

2 egg whites, beaten to stiff peaks

21-oz. can your favorite pie filling

Mix graham cracker crumbs, brown sugar and margarine in bowl until crumbly.
Press evenly on bottom and sides of 9-inch pie pan.

Beat cream cheese until light and fluffy. Blend in sugar and vanilla. Fold in beaten egg whites.
Spoon mixture into prepared crust. Bake at 325°F for 20 to 25 minutes or until filling is set.
Allow to cool before topping with pie filling or fruit variations (below).

VARIATION: FRESH FRUIT TOPPING

4 c. fresh fruit of your choice

1 c. juice from above-mentioned fruit (you may need 2 more cups of fresh fruit to liquify in blender)

½ c. sugar

2 T. cornstarch

Arrange fruit on cooled cream cheese cake. Blend juice, sugar and cornstarch in saucepan.
Cook at medium heat until thick. Spoon sauce over fruit. Cover and chill or freeze.

Tip: Canned fruit can be substituted for fresh fruit. You will need 1 to 2 (16-oz.) cans crushed pineapple. Drain and reserve juice, and add 1 to 2 drops food coloring, if desired.

Lewis Newell
Cassopolis, MI

WOODWORKING WITH RECLAIMED MATERIALS

Six Board Box

Editor's Note: The woodworking projects shown on these pages were all created by Member Roger Russell of Anderson Island, Washington. Roger has a great talent for making beautiful objects from salvaged or overlooked material—one of the signature abilities of the true handyman.

BAND ORGAN

This project is an original design for a merry-go-round organ. It is 6 ft. 8 in. high x 4 ft. wide x 18 in. deep. It operates using punched cardboard books and four 18-in. x 12-in. bellows. It has 56 pipes in octave pairs. All the gold rounds on the front were made by resawing croquet balls. Other parts are 3/4-in. pine, cut with a jig saw. The pipes were rebuilt from leftovers after a restoration of a church organ. It is loaded with enough music to run perhaps 90 minutes before repeating.

SPALTED ALDER & CEDAR CHEST

I built this chest with a cedar frame and spalted alder panels from trees in my back yard. It is 20 in. high x 18 in. wide x 38 in. long. All corner joints are mitered and the sides are made with basic frame-and-panel construction. It has a plywood bottom. I finished it with satin tung oil, then rubbed out the finish with 0000 steel wool.

SIX BOARD BOX

I made this chest from one board that was 16 in. wide x 16 ft. long. The board was left in the woods in the early 40s, when the local cedar was harvested for use in the war effort. The 30-in. buttresses were discarded and ignored until last year. They had almost no rot! I cut the slab into inch-thick boards. This box is 37 in. long x 18 in. wide x 20 in. high. It is finished with lacquer and paste wax. I made two for my neighbor's two little girls (they were his logs).

Spalted Alder & Cedar Chest

OBELISK CLOCK

Made of spalted alder and walnut, this clock is 22 in. high x 22 in. wide x 7 in. deep. The damp Northwest is perfect for the spalting of alder and maple. I take full advantage of this beautiful wood for many projects, trim, boxes, instrument veneer, mantles, frames, cabinets, and other decorative items. The clock is finished with satin tung oil.

Band Organ

Obelisk Clock

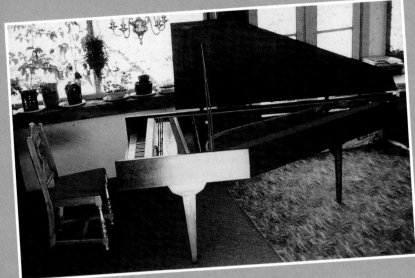
Grand Piano

GRAND PIANO

This eight-foot-long, 35-in.-wide grand piano has leather covered hammers, felt dampers, polished fir naturals, stained Dogwood sharps, an all-white-pine case with fir frame, solid oak wrestplank and re-used, sandblasted tuning pins. The bridge and nut are apple wood, which is very hard and right for the job. The sounding board is made from birch door skin, well ribbed with spruce. Everything was lacquered and rubbed to a high polish.

When played, one heard more wood than wire, so the piano was made over into a really good sounding harpsichord, which it remains today.

ITALIAN HARPSICHORD, NUMBER 13

The case for this Italian harpsichord is 1/4-in. birch plywood, veneered with old oak taken from a piano case. It has a typical Italian frame of 1/2-in. fir with a hitch pin rail on the bentside made from laminated maple. The keys are made from clear white pine, glued into a panel, veneered with freeze dried Madrona, then cut with band saw and coping saw to shape. The strings are drawn steel wire .010-in. to .025-in. thick. The bridge and nut are California eucalyptus. The sounding board is perfect straight-grained fir and well supported by spruce ribs. Wrestplank is 1 1/4-in. oak. Interior is bird's-eye maple like the name board. It is finished with apple wax. The sound is bright, and the action is quick and reliable.

Roger Russell
Anderson Island, WA

Italian Harpsichord

Honey Apple Pie

Crust (Makes 2)

1 tsp. salt

5 T. milk

3 T. honey

1 c. shortening

3 c. flour

FILLING

½ c. sugar

1 tsp. cinnamon

3 T. lemon juice

½ c. honey

2 T. flour

¼ tsp. salt

¼ tsp. cloves

¼ tsp. allspice

5 medium apples, peeled and sliced

Margarine

Prepare crust: mix salt, milk and honey together and add to shortening. Cut this into flour until dough is smooth but do not over mix. Form a ball with dough. Wrap in plastic wrap and place in refrigerator.
For filling: Combine sugar, cinnamon, lemon juice, honey, flour, salt, cloves, allspice and apples in bowl. Divide dough into 2 equal portions. Prepare bottom crust and place in medium pie pan. Place apples evenly on crust and dot with margarine. Fit and seal upper crust. Make slits on top crust for steam to escape. Dot top with thin slices of margarine. Sprinkle 1 tablespoon sugar over top. Bake at 425°F for 35 to 45 minutes or until apples are tender.

Gary Mallon
Post Falls, ID

Georgia's Chocolate Fudge

⅓ c. cocoa

3 c. sugar

⅛ tsp. salt

1½ c. milk

¼ c. margarine

1 tsp. vanilla

Combine cocoa, sugar and salt in large saucepan. Add milk gradually, mix thoroughly. Bring to bubbly boil on high heat, stirring constantly. Reduce heat to medium and continue to boil without stirring until it reaches 243°F (soft-ball stage). Be sure bulb of thermometer is not resting on bottom of pan. Remove saucepan from heat. Add margarine and vanilla to mixture. Beat mixture by hand until it thickens and loses gloss. Quickly pour into buttered pan.

VARIATIONS
Popcorn Fudge: Add 1 ½ to 2 cups ground popped corn with the margarine and vanilla.

Walnut Fudge, Coconut Fudge, etc.: Use whatever you want, adding 1 ½ to 2 cups of your choice.

Lewis Newell
Cassopolis, MI

Homemade Hot Chocolate Mix

5 c. dry milk

6 oz. dry coffee creamer

1 c. powdered sugar

2 c. dry chocolate drink mix

Mix dry milk, creamer, sugar and drink mix. Store in airtight container. Use ⅓ cup mix to 1 cup hot water. Top with marshmallows.

David Kline
Sugarcreek, OH

Pecan Tassies

½ c. butter

3-oz. cream cheese

1 c. flour

4 T. butter, melted

1½ c. light brown sugar, packed

2 eggs, lightly beaten

1 c. chopped pecans

Cut ½ cup butter and cream cheese into flour to form pastry. Roll into 24 to 36 balls and chill for 1 hour or more. Place each ball in a miniature muffin tin and, using your thumb, press it into the cup and up the sides. Be careful not to tear pastry.

Blend together 4 tablespoons melted butter, brown sugar, eggs and pecans. Spoon filling into each pastry cup. Bake at 350°F for 20 minutes. While tassies are still hot, run a sharp knife around edges and pop them out of tins. Tassies can be individually wrapped and frozen for 1 month.

Donna Miller
Collierville, TN

Pecan Tassies

Crustless Coconut Pie

1 c. milk

1 c. sugar

¼ c. melted butter

½ tsp. baking powder

Pinch salt

1 c. coconut, flaked or shredded

¼ c. flour

½ tsp. vanilla

2 eggs, beaten

Mix milk, sugar, butter, baking powder, salt, coconut, flour, vanilla and eggs together and pour into ungreased pie pan. Bake at 350°F for 35 to 45 minutes until top is golden brown or butter knife inserted in center comes out clean.

Sharon Matheny
Van Wert, OH

Cheesecake Torte

2 c. crushed graham crackers

1 c. flour

¾ c. butter, melted

8-oz. tub whipped topping

1 c. powdered sugar

8 oz. cream cheese, softened

21-oz.can cherry, apple, blueberry or your choice pie filling

Prepare crust: Combine graham crackers, flour and butter and press into 9 x 13-inch cake pan. Bake at 350°F for 9 to 12 minutes. Allow crust to cool. Beat whipped topping, powdered sugar and cream cheese together until well blended. Pour filling mixture into cool crust. Top with pie filling. Chill for several hours before serving.

Rhonda Bahr
Medford, WI

Piña Colada Punch

1½ (69 oz.) cans pineapple juice

15 oz. cream of coconut

1 qt. vanilla ice cream

12 liter ginger ale

Mix pineapple juice and cream of coconut with wire whisk or beater; blend in softened ice cream. Add ginger ale.

David Kline
Sugarcreek, OH

Mock Raspberry Jam

4 to 6 c. green tomatoes

1 pkg. raspberry gelatin

Sugar to taste (jam will be less sweet when cooled, so use extra)

Grind tomatoes through meat grinder, blender or other such appliance. Put in pot and bring to boil. Add gelatin and sugar. Skim foam from top. Place in jars and seal with wax. It will taste like it was made with raspberries.

Jen Jimison
Louisville, OH

RETAINING WALL

Before

When I built my house I told the builder I wanted a retaining wall that would be nice looking and also be suitable for planting with flowers. I didn't realize his opinion and mine would be so different. I lived with the wall he built for four years but I was never happy with it.

The 6-in-square timbers on the wall he built ranged from 6 to 8 ft. in length. The slope of the wall was so great that any plants other than ivy would fall out. So I decided to replace the wall. Because there was no access space for equipment I had to do all the work using only a wheelbarrow. I removed the old timbers and most of the dirt backfill. I carted in the interlocking wall blocks, drainage rock and new backfill for the new wall.

The wall I built split the slope into two levels. The lower wall is about 3 ft. high and the upper wall is about 4 ft. high. I created a setback between the upper and lower walls for planting flowers. The total length is close to 80 ft. One of the largest problems I had was dealing with buried boulders. Several were too large to remove, so I had to break them up with an impact drill, hammer and chisel. The project took over a year to finish.

Gene Presson
Raleigh, NC

Editor's Note: Gene's ambitious project uses a good method for dealing with steep slopes: stepping back a retaining wall into multiple walls to handle the incline. Shorter walls, in general, undergo less stress, are not as likely to collapse and pose less of a safety hazard. In fact, many building codes require that you get a special permit to build any wall that's more than 3 ft. tall—check with your local building department.

Apple Coffee Cake

Grasshopper Pie

20-oz. bag Oreo Cookies
½ c. butter, melted
10-oz. bag large marshmallows
½ c. milk
4 T. creme de menthe syrup
2 c. whipped topping

Scrape frosting off cookies. Reserve frosting and crush cookies. Soften cookie frosting and butter in microwave for 10 seconds. Add frosting mixture to crushed cookies; mix well. Reserve ¼ cup of crumbs; press remaining crumbs into 9 x 13-inch pan. Chill crust.

Melt marshmallows with milk. Cool. Add syrup and whipped topping to marshmallow sauce. Pour sauce over crust and top with reserved crumbs. Chill before serving.

Amy Jo Gross
Bismarck, ND

Apple Coffee Cake

1½ c. apples, peeled, cored and chopped
½ c. nuts, chopped
⅓ c. sugar
1 tsp. pumpkin pie spice
3 c. baking mix
2 eggs, beaten
¼ c. butter or margarine, melted
¼ c. milk
½ c. powdered sugar
2 to 3 tsp. milk

Combine apples, nuts, sugar and pie spice. Mix baking mix, eggs, butter and ¼ cup milk. Beat 20 strokes by hand with spoon or whisk. Turn onto lightly floured surface; knead 8 to 10 times. Roll into 9 x 13-inch rectangle. Spread apple mixture to within ½ inch of edges. Beginning at narrow side, roll up jelly roll style. Pinch edges into roll. Place seam side down in greased 9 x 5-inch loaf pan. Bake for 1 hour at 350°F. Remove from pan immediately. Cool slightly. Combine powdered sugar and 2 to 3 teaspoons milk until smooth and of desired consistency. Drizzle over warm loaf. Slice to serve.

Gene M. Bryant
Greensburg, KY

Bread Pudding

9 to 12 slices bread
3 eggs
½ tsp. salt
2 tsp. vanilla
¾ c. sugar
2¼ c. milk
1 tsp. cinnamon
1½ tsp. margarine

RUM SAUCE
½ c. cream or whole milk
1 c. sugar
½ c. butter, melted
1 tsp. rum or vanilla

Slice bread slices into half-inch strips. Place strips lattice-fashion in 11 x 7-inch baking pan. Combine eggs, salt, vanilla, sugar, milk, cinnamon and margarine. Pour half of egg mixture over bread. Cover with lattice-fashion layer of bread strips. Pour remaining egg mixture over bread. Set baking dish in pan of 1-inch-deep hot water. Bake at 325°F in center of oven for 1 hour or until lightly brown.

Prepare rum sauce: Mix cream and sugar in saucepan. Heat cream mixture but do not boil. Beat in butter and stir into rum sauce.

Mary Gross
Bismarck, ND

Index